THE ULTIMATE FIX

The Parasympathetic Mind

DR. MANSI PRABHAVALKAR

This is a work of nonfiction. The events and the incidents mentioned in the book are true and real. However, some names and characteristics have been changed, some events have been compressed, and some dialogues have been recreated.

First Edition: December 2025
Printed in India

Printed at: Gapmeta Ventures Pvt.Ltd, Mumbai
Typeset in Times New Roman

ISBN: 978-93-6070-848-1

Cover Design: Prajakta Sawant

STORYMIRROR
Stories that reflect you

Publisher: StoryMirror Infotech Pvt. Ltd.
Unit No-F/705, 7th Floor, Kailas Corporate Lounge,
Veer Savarkar Road, Vikhroli Park Site,
Vikhroli West, Mumbai-400079,
Maharashtra, India.

Web: storymirror.com
Facebook: @storymirror
Twitter: @story_mirror
Instagram: @storymirror
Email: marketing@storymirror.com

PROLOGUE: THE PURPOSE OF LIFE

LIFE IS A journey, unfolding in ways we may never fully understand. At its core, we seek happiness, the truth and the steps we must take to find it. We search for meaning, a reason to exist, and a sense of purpose. In Sanskrit, this quest is known as Dharma; in Japanese, it's called Ikigai, the purpose of life.

But have we ever paused to ask ourselves: What is it that I am truly searching for? How do I want to live this life?

So many of us walk through this world lost in an illusion, trapped by the confusion of not knowing who we truly are. I still find myself questioning: Who am I? We spend our lives building connections, yet the first one we establish is often with our body. We feel so deeply connected to this physical form that we believe we are the body. And because of this, we dedicate ourselves to nurturing it, feeding it, and acquiring more for it. Our world becomes a search for possessions, pleasure, and status, all of which are meant to fulfill the body but not the soul.

The truth is, the very idea of who we are is borrowed. It's shaped by the people around us, those who themselves may be just as lost as we are. The labels we wear and the identities we claim are often reflections of how others perceive us. And those perceptions are not truths, but projections of their own experiences, mind-sets, and judgments, shaped by their unsorted pasts. We internalize those labels, letting them form the image we have of ourselves. But in doing so, we may forget that those perceptions are just illusions, distorted by others' perceptions, not our own truth.

Perhaps it's time to ask ourselves: What if we are not who they say we are? What if who we are is something far deeper, far more expansive than we have ever imagined?

MY JOURNEY

My journey has been one of transformation, a path that took me from a pale moon in the dark sky to a shining sun. This evolution has played a significant role in shaping who I am today and how others perceive me.

The Legacy I Inherited:

I am Dr. Mansi Prabhavalkar. I was born as Mona Trivedi on September 14, 1969, into a Hindu Brahmin family. My upbringing was influenced by the values of honor, service, and duty, values deeply ingrained in me by my family. My father, Capt. H.C. Trivedi, served in the Indian Army, a man who fought with courage and determination in the 1965 India-Pakistan War. His spirit of service and sacrifice shaped not only my life but also the way I understood the world around me.

Another defining figure in my life was my uncle, Mr. Brajesh Chandra Mishra. An Indian diplomat and politician, he served as Principal Secretary to Prime Minister Atal Bihari Vajpayee, and later became India's first National Security Advisor. His contributions to India's foreign policy earned him the prestigious Padma Bhushan.

Growing up in such a family, I witnessed a life dedicated to public service, leadership, and a profound sense of responsibility.

Capt. H. C. Trivedi

Mr Brajesh Mishra

But as I reflect on this journey, it is clear that while I have inherited many legacies, the most powerful transformation I have undergone is in the one I've chosen to create for myself. It is in moving beyond the labels and identities given to me and discovering the true light within me. My path has been one of awakening to my own purpose and the limitless potential within.

Mumbai: The Birthplace of My Purpose:

My journey truly began in the vibrant, bustling streets of Mumbai, where I spent the early years of my life. It was here that I first experienced the joy and fulfillment of helping others as I ran my private medical practice. The long hours, the connection with patients, the sense of purpose in offering care, it all shaped who I was, and for a long time, I felt grounded in the work I was doing. My practice wasn't just a career; it was my calling, a way to contribute to the community I loved, to make a difference, and to witness first-hand the human stories that would come through my door.

Crossing Shores: The Move to Dubai:

But life, as it often does, led me to unexpected changes. In 2004, a new chapter unfolded when I decided to move to Dubai. Leaving Mumbai, my home, was one of the most difficult choices I've ever made. It wasn't just a physical move; it felt like a piece of my heart was being left behind. I was leaving the comfort of familiarity, the support of close-knit relationships, and the life I had carefully built.

Dubai was an entirely different world, fast-paced, ambitious, and full of possibilities, but also starkly unfamiliar. I stepped into this new chapter with both excitement and uncertainty. The transition wasn't easy. I missed the connections I had with my patients in Mumbai, the deep sense of satisfaction I had found in the medical field. But I soon realized that while I may have left one life behind, a new one was waiting for me to embrace it, to grow, and to explore a different side of myself.

In the Corporate World: Lessons Beyond Medicine:

Though it was hard to let go of what I had known, my move to Dubai opened new doors and allowed me to experience a different side of healthcare, the corporate world, a place I never thought I would find myself. And while it was a shift from what I had envisioned for my life, I began to see that the lessons, the experiences, and the people I met along the way would shape me in ways I could never have imagined back in Mumbai. The journey was one of immense personal growth, but it was also a reminder that sometimes we need to let go of the old to make space for the new.

The Body Speaks: My Health Became My Teacher:

I had always taken pride in being physically fit, feeling strong and healthy, until life took a sudden turn. Hypertension, Hyperlipidaemia, and Hypothyroidism crept into my life like uninvited guests. It was a jarring shift. For years, I had been accustomed to pushing myself, always being in control, but now my body was sending me signals that I couldn't ignore. Despite my health challenges, I continued my journey in the corporate world, immersing myself in the high-paced, demanding environment of the healthcare industry in Dubai. I was an Insurance Manager and Clinical Auditor for over 13 years, a role that gave me a sense of purpose, but, at the same time, added layers of stress that I didn't fully understand.

Awakening: The Turning Point with Sister Shivani:

Then came the turning point. In 2016, I watched a video by Brahmakumari Sister Shivani. Her words were simple yet profound. It was as though something deep within me was being awakened. She spoke about the power of thoughts, how they are energy, how they shape our lives and impact every cell in our body. I had never heard anything like it before. It resonated with me in ways I couldn't fully explain at that moment, but something shifted inside. I was still in the corporate world, but now I began to question everything I had believed about myself, my health, and my relationships.

Sister Shivani

I began to realize that I had been outsourcing my happiness and blaming external circumstances for my stress and frustration. But Sister Shivani's words made me see the truth: I was the creator of my thoughts, feelings, and reactions. No one else could dictate my inner peace, and it was up to me to take full responsibility for my mind and my body.

Healing from Within: Mind Over Matter

The change was gradual but powerful. I started noticing a profound shift in my relationships with colleagues. My approach to life became more gentle, compassionate, and understanding. I no longer reacted to challenges with anger or frustration but with calmness and acceptance. The idea that "thought is karma" became my guiding principle. I realized that every thought, no matter how small, was a choice, a choice that could either empower me or drain me.

While the health challenges I faced didn't disappear overnight, I began to feel a sense of balance and peace within myself that I hadn't felt before. I am no longer at war with myself or the world around me. I am learning to embrace my responsibility, to cultivate my thoughts with intention, and to honor my body as the temple it is. The journey has been one of self-discovery and transformation. While it hasn't been easy, I am grateful for the lessons that have come my way.

I've always believed that discipline and dedication are the keys to success, especially growing up in an army family, where structure and commitment were instilled in me from an early age. For 25 years, I held onto a deeply ingrained routine, waking up at 3 a.m., practicing yoga and pranayama, and then heading to bed by 9 p.m. Every day, without fail. It wasn't just a habit but a lifestyle I had committed to with every fiber of my being. It became a part of me, a constant reminder that true well-being requires unwavering dedication.

But even with this disciplined approach to physical health, I faced battles that no amount of physical routine could cure hypertension, hyperlipidemia, and hypothyroidism. They were constant reminders that the body's well-being isn't just about what we do physically, but also about what we carry within. So, I took it a step further, working deeply not just on my body, but on my mind. I began to truly take care of my thoughts, realizing that my mental and emotional state had a direct impact on my physical health. The more I embraced this inner work, the more it felt like I was healing in every sense of the word.

Four years later, the results of my dedication were nothing short of miraculous. My lab results, those constant markers of my chronic ailments, began to return to normal. It was as though my body had finally aligned with my inner light and I was healing from the inside out. And now, it's been four years since I stopped my medications. It's not just the absence of pills that feels significant, but the peace of mind, the sense of control, and the deep trust I now have in my body's ability to heal and thrive.

This journey hasn't been easy, and there were moments of doubt and struggle. But through it all, I've learned that true healing comes from within, from the thoughts we nurture, the habits we cultivate, and the faith we place in ourselves. It's been a humble and beautiful reminder that with discipline, dedication, and self-awareness, we can overcome even the most daunting challenges.

The Law of Karma: A Lesson in Forgiveness

Then came another turning point. It was a moment that shook my world. I was walking through the mall, and a lady in a wheelchair inadvertently rammed the foot end of her chair into my right ankle, severing my Achilles tendon by 60%. The pain was excruciating, and the reality that I needed immediate surgery to repair the damage set in. Suddenly, I found myself bound to a wheelchair for three long months, completely dependent on others. It felt like my world had turned upside down.

But in the midst of this, something remarkable happened. I had been walking a path of self-actualization, learning to cultivate peace and acceptance in my life. And when this unexpected event struck, I found the courage to let go of any bitterness or anger. I remembered a lesson I had learned, the Law of Karma: Whatever I receive in this life, I must have given at some point. If what I received wasn't something I liked or wanted, it was a result of something I had sent out into the universe before. If I haven't liked what I've received, I need to ask for forgiveness for whatever I have sent. That's a vibration of purification. Forgiveness (both seeking and giving) dissolves karmic knots. It frees energy that was once stuck in resentment or judgment.

I realized that I had to take responsibility for my own actions, and that included the way I responded to what was happening in my life. So, I sat in meditation, reflecting deeply on the incident. I asked for forgiveness, not only for the woman who had unknowingly caused my injury but for myself as well, for any wrongs I had ever done. I understood that my situation was a reflection of something I had contributed to in the past, and I had the power to change the energy I was sending out.

In that moment, I made a decision: I would not raise a single question in my mind about the episode. No anger, no resentment, no regret. I chose to accept what had happened as part of my journey. The path of forgiveness and self-awareness wasn't always easy, but it was the one that led to healing, not just physically, but emotionally and spiritually as well.

From Pain to Purpose:

That experience, painful as it was, taught me one of the most profound lessons of my life: that we are the creators of our experiences, and by choosing to send out positive energy, we can change the course of our lives. With each step of healing, I found myself growing stronger, not just in my body, but in my mind and spirit. I no longer saw myself as a victim of circumstances, but as a soul on a journey, learning and evolving with every experience.

After that life-altering episode, I found myself facing a series of challenges in my professional life that felt overwhelming. The injury, the time in a wheelchair, the recovery, it all triggered something deeper within me, a realization that the physical and emotional wounds I had been carrying needed more than just external healing. It was in the depths of these struggles that I made a decision that would change the course of my life: I decided to pursue spiritual well-being, to embark on a path of true inner healing.

The Seeker and the Student:

I began taking wellness courses, immersing myself in learning about the power of the mind and spirit. Over time, these teachings transformed me, and before I knew it, I had accumulated 22 certifications in various wellness fields. But more than just a collection of certificates, each course was a step in my personal journey, a journey of awakening, of seeking answers to questions that had lingered in my heart for so long. And through this, I discovered the profound power of meditation, the path to Swarajya, Swa Pe Rajya, which means "winning over the self."

The Birth of Seraphicheal: Lightness as Healing:

It was this inner quest, this journey of meditation and self-discovery that ignited the creation of my webpage, SERAPHICHEAL. The name "Seraphic" holds a deep meaning for me. It comes from the word "angel," a being often depicted with wings. But then I asked myself, do angels have wings? In reality, when the mind and body are light, when we let go of the weight we carry from hurt, grief, and trauma, we can feel as though we are soaring, free from the burdens that once held us down.

For so long, we've carried the heaviness of our past experiences, and this emotional weight makes our minds and bodies heavy. We neglect our health, and it shows in the disease and weight we struggle with. But Seraphicheal is a mission to help others lighten that load. It's about offering tools to heal the mind, nourish the body, and reclaim the lightness we're meant to feel. When we can let go of what weighs us down, we can truly fly, like angels, free and unburdened.

This physical, emotional, and spiritual healing journey has been nothing short of transformative. I am no longer just surviving life, but living with purpose and grace. Through Seraphicheal, I hope to share these tools, these teachings, and the gift of lightness, so that others too can take flight, leaving behind the weight of their past and embracing the freedom of their true selves.

TABLE OF CONTENTS

CHAPTER 1

THE ULTIMATE FIX – HEALING THE MIND AND BODY

THE CONCEPT OF "The Ultimate Fix", what does it mean? What are we truly seeking to heal, and where does this healing come from? As I discovered on my journey, the answer is this: *Healing must happen at two levels, both the outer body and the inner mind.*

The Illusion of Physical Health:

For so long, I, like many others, believed that true health was simply about how well our bodies functioned. We measure our health by how we feel physically, by the signs and symptoms we experience, by the results of our laboratory tests, by how strong or fit we appear. If our bodies seemed to work well, we believed we were healthy.

But what I came to understand is that this is only part of the picture. Health isn't just about what's happening physically; it's about the mind, too. We often forget that our thoughts, emotions, and internal state have a powerful impact on our overall well-being. The truth is, you can be physically fit, but if your mind is clouded with stress, anxiety, or unresolved emotional pain, your health will never be whole. Our inner world directly influences our outer world, and both must be healed for true wellness to occur.

Medicine or Maintenance:

For so long, we have lived in a world where health was measured by numbers, lab results, blood pressure. If those numbers weren't within the "normal" range, the solution was clear: visit the physician, take the prescribed medications, and try to keep the disease in check. And so, we would find ourselves relying on these medications, each pill an attempt to control the symptoms and maintain a sense of stability.

But something always nagged at me, deep down. While the medications kept the numbers under control, they never really healed. They never addressed the root of ailments. Modern medicine, as miraculous as it is, often only manages the disease, rather than eradicating it. The disease would always return when the medications stopped.

We weren't being healed in the truest sense. We were simply being maintained. The levels in the body were being controlled, but they weren't truly being balanced. The underlying cause of the imbalances, whether physical or emotional, remained unaddressed.

It was about understanding that true healing comes when we address both the body and the mind. When we work on healing our emotions, our thoughts, and our lifestyle, we create lasting change that doesn't just mask the symptoms but brings about real transformation. And while I will forever be grateful for the advancements of modern medicine, I have come to realize that the true path to wellness is a holistic one, one that combines medical care with deep self-care, compassion, and the courage to heal from within.

The Power of Perception:

There was a time, not so long ago, when a blood pressure of 120/90 mmHg was considered normal. We lived our lives with a sense of security, believing that this number was just a part of our routine health checks. Everyone felt at ease. After all, we trusted the system, trusted the definitions and labels that were handed to us. But then, something shifted. That same blood pressure reading, once deemed perfectly normal, was suddenly labeled as "borderline," and overnight, panic began to spread. People rushed to doctors, to specialists, worried that they were on the verge of something dangerous. Cardiac cases started rising, and the fear of an impending heart attack or stroke became a daily concern for many.

But what changed? Was it really the number? Or was it the way our minds began to interpret that number? When we were told 120/90 was normal, we accepted it without question. Our minds were at peace. There was no doubt, no anxiety. But when the definition changed, when we were told it was "borderline," that's when everything shifted. It wasn't just the blood pressure reading that changed. It was the doubt that was planted in our minds. The fear crept in, and with it came stress, worry, and panic.

When the Mind Creates the Disease:

It was at that moment I realized how powerful the mind truly is. A simple number, a shift in perspective, could create a cascade of emotional and physiological responses that impact our health. The power of our thoughts, our beliefs, and our fears could shape our reality in ways we never fully understood before.

It made me reflect on how much control we have over our health, not just through physical measures, but through our mindset. The fear we carry and the doubts we entertain, can manifest in our bodies in ways that we may not even realize. What if, instead of fearing "borderline" readings, we learned to embrace our health with a sense of peace, trust, and balance? What if we remembered that our thoughts directly impact our bodies?

Ultimately, this experience taught me one of the most profound lessons: the mind and body are inseparable. Our beliefs, fears, and anxieties shape our health just as much as physical factors do. Only by addressing both the body and the mind, with awareness and compassion, can we truly find healing.

The Root Cause Lies Within:

It's a harsh truth, but one that we can no longer ignore: if the root cause of a disease is not addressed, it will find its way back, no matter how many times we try to fix the symptoms. Take, for example, the case of a blocked artery. Modern medicine has given us the powerful tool of interventional procedures, like stenting, to rectify the immediate issue. These procedures can offer a sense of relief and even save lives. And for a while, everything may seem fine, the problem is resolved, the block is cleared, and we can breathe easy again.

But what happens when we don't address the underlying cause, the deep-rooted habits, emotions, or imbalances that led to that blockage in the first place? If we only focus on fixing the surface-level issue, the disease will have no choice but to resurface somewhere else. It might emerge in a different artery, a different organ, or a different part of our body. The physical ailment may shift, but the underlying issue remains.

This is the power of true healing: it's not just about fixing what is broken on the outside; it's about addressing the root cause, transforming the energy that flows within, and allowing that transformation to ripple outward. Only then can we break free from the cycle of disease and truly thrive.

The Healing Power of Belief:

It's a question that many of us have wondered about at some point: Why do two individuals with the same disease, even taking the same medication, experience such different recoveries? One person seems to bounce back quickly, their healing almost effortless, while the other seems to struggle, their progress slow and uncertain. It's perplexing, isn't it? But when you dive deeper, you begin to realize that the answer lies not just in the medicine or the treatment, but in the power of belief, the state of mind.

The person who recovers quickly, who seems to heal almost effortlessly, is the one who has full faith in the treatment, and who believes wholeheartedly in his or her healing journey. Their mind is positive, optimistic, and open to the idea that they will get better.

This belief, this trust in the process, becomes a powerful force in their recovery. They are not only taking the medicine, they are embracing it, allowing it to work, and trusting that they are on the path to wellness.

But for the person who struggles, the one who is slow to recover, his or her journey is clouded with doubt and dissatisfaction. Perhaps they question the treatment or fear that it won't work, or maybe they are simply weighed down by negative thoughts. The mind is filled with uncertainty and worry, which blocks the natural flow of healing. This doubt creates an emotional barrier, preventing the body from responding as quickly to the treatment. It goes to show that so much of our recovery depends not just on the physical factors, but on the mindset we bring to the table.

The Concept of "Dis-ease":

And that's when the disease concept takes on a whole new meaning. The word itself, "*disease*", can be understood in two ways: as a physical illness or condition, and as a state of dis-ease in the mind. When the mind is at dis-ease, in turmoil, filled with fear, anger, or uncertainty, it manifests in the body as disease. Our thoughts and emotions create the environment in which illness either thrives or heals. True healing is not just about what we take into our bodies, but what we feed our minds and souls.

The Sacred Midline: The Body's Central Axis of Energy:

When we pause to reflect on the human body, something truly profound becomes apparent. Imagine a straight line drawn from the top of your head, all the way down to the lower part of your abdomen, to the very center of your being. This line, the midline of the body, is not just a simple path, it is the central axis of your entire existence. It is where the heart of your being resides, where the energy flows most powerfully.

As we trace this line, we begin to realize something remarkable: the major organs of our body fall along this very midline. From the brain to the heart, to the lungs, the stomach, and down to the reproductive organs and the anus, each of these vital parts is aligned with this sacred line. These organs, so integral to our survival, to our vitality, to our very being, depend on a steady and harmonious supply of blood, energy, and communication through nerves and vessels. And it is along this midline that the major pathways of life flow, nourishing, sustaining, and connecting us to our inner power.

What's even more powerful is the recognition that these very points along the midline, this sacred line of life, are often considered the centers of energy in many spiritual traditions. These centers are called Chakras. Each Chakra corresponds to a different aspect of our being, our physical health, our emotional well-being, our sense of purpose, and our spiritual connection. When these Chakras are aligned and balanced, the body and mind flow in harmony, and we experience a deep sense of wellness and peace.

But when these Chakras are blocked or out of balance, it affects not just our physical health, but our mental, emotional, and spiritual state. The energy that should be flowing freely through our body becomes stagnant, and that stagnation can manifest as disease, pain, or dis-ease in our lives. This is why nurturing and aligning these energy centers is so vital, not just for healing, but for creating a life of balance, joy, and purpose.

In my journey, I have come to see these Chakras not just as abstract concepts but as the very lifelines of my existence. They remind me that we are so much more than just flesh and bone. We are energy, interconnected, vibrating with the very essence of life. When we honor and align these centers, we tap into a deeper, more powerful healing force within ourselves.

The Nervous System: The Body's Electrical Symphony:

When I reflect on the intricate beauty of our body's design, I can't help but marvel at the wisdom of how everything is interconnected. Our nervous system, this remarkable web of life, carries the very essence of our being from one point to another. It's like an endless flow of energy, transmitting signals, thoughts, and emotions throughout every inch of our body. From one nerve cell to the next, through the synaptic junctions, this energy is passed along, guiding us, protecting us, and allowing us to experience the world.

The nervous system is like the body's electrical grid, and it is divided into two broad parts. The Central Nervous System, which is composed of the brain and the spinal cord, acts as the command center. It's here that all the impulses begin, the thoughts, the decisions, and the responses. The brain sends signals to the entire body, telling us how to move, how to react, and how to feel. It's the powerhouse of our consciousness, the very core of who we are.

And then, there is the Peripheral Nervous System, which acts like the vast network of roads that connect the central command to the rest of the body. It has two key divisions: the Sympathetic Nervous System and the Parasympathetic Nervous System. The Sympathetic system is like the body's "accelerator," constantly on alert, preparing us for action, for fight or flight. It's what kicks in when we face stress, danger, or excitement. It gets our heart racing, our senses heightened, ready to respond.

On the other hand, the Parasympathetic Nervous System is like the "brakes," the calming force that tells us it's time to rest, to heal, to digest, to find peace. It's the part that helps us relax after stress, guiding us back to balance and harmony.

When I reflect on this balance between the two, I realize just how crucial it is for our well-being. Too much activity from the Sympathetic system, without the calming influence of the Parasympathetic system, leaves us in a state of constant stress, tension, and dis-ease. But when both systems are balanced, when we allow ourselves to respond to life's challenges with grace and calm, and we give ourselves permission to rest and rejuvenate, the body finds harmony.

This balance is not just physical. It's emotional, too. Our nervous system is constantly responding not just to external stimuli but to our thoughts and emotions. How we process stress, how we let go of tension, how we heal from trauma, it all flows through this system. And just as we nurture our physical health, we must nurture our nervous system with mindfulness, relaxation, and self-compassion.

Our mind and body are constantly in conversation, and the state of our nervous system can profoundly impact our emotional and physical well-being. It's a call to pay attention, to listen to the subtle signals our body is giving us, and to take steps toward finding peace and balance within ourselves. Because when the nervous system is aligned, when the energy flows freely, we experience a deep sense of vitality, healing, and wholeness.

The Cortisol Connection:

When we experience stress, when we are frightened or anxious, it's as though we are sending a signal to our body that there is danger that we need to fight or flee. This is where the Sympathetic Nervous System comes into play. It is the body's natural response to stress, preparing us for battle, heightening our senses, and propelling us into action. This is the Fight-or-Flight response, a mechanism designed for our survival in moments of acute danger.

But here's where the complexity of human existence lies: in our modern world, stress is not always an external threat. So much of it comes from within us, our worries, our fears, our unresolved emotional trauma. And when we constantly live in this heightened state, the sympathetic nervous system stays activated. Over time, this triggers the release of cortisol, the stress hormone, flooding our bodies with chemicals meant to help us cope with immediate danger. The problem is, when these levels of Cortisol remain high for too long, they begin to wear down our systems. It causes degeneration of our cells.

One of the most insidious effects of prolonged stress is its impact on our blood vessels. cortisol causes the hardening of the arteries, this is known as atherosclerosis. The blood vessels, once flexible and vital, begin to stiffen, narrowing the pathways through which life-giving blood flows to our organs. As the heart struggles to pump blood through these hardened arteries, it has to work harder and harder. Over time, the very cells that once thrived begin to suffer. And that suffering extends to the organs that rely on these cells for nourishment and function.

The most heartbreaking part of this process is the emotional trauma we carry, often unaddressed, piling up, layer by layer, over the years. The unresolved pain, fears, emotional wounds we haven't healed from, contribute to the endless rise of cortisol in our system. And as the years pass by, this stress and emotional burden doesn't just affect our minds, it begins to manifest physically in ways we can no longer ignore. It is no longer just a temporary feeling of unease; it becomes a full-blown disease.

But we can release the grip of stress, heal from our emotional wounds, and reduce the cortisol levels that are wreaking havoc on our bodies. It starts with awareness, with understanding that we are not helpless in the face of stress. We can make choices to heal, through mindfulness, meditation, therapy, self-compassion, and love. We can shift from living in a constant state of fear to one of peace, allowing our bodies to heal and our hearts to find balance.

This journey is not always easy, but it is so worth it. When we choose to heal emotionally, we give our bodies the opportunity to heal physically. And in that healing, we find the true restoration of health, vitality, and peace.

This understanding has touched me deeply, because it brings to light a truth I had never fully realized before: the physical manifestation of disease is not always immediate. It doesn't happen overnight. The body doesn't simply break down without reason. It is a reflection of what has been brewing in the mind for a long time. When the mind holds on to stress, fear, anxiety, unresolved trauma, or emotional pain over a long period of time, it creates an internal injury. This mental injury, this ongoing state of dis-ease, eventually manifests in the body, sometimes years later, as physical disease. It's like a silent storm that brews within, and we only see the destruction after it's too late.

The realization that the body's disease is merely a symptom of a much deeper mental struggle has been a life-changing epiphany for me. It made me reflect on how we often ignore our emotional well-being, pushing ourselves to "be strong" and "carry on" despite the mental injuries we accumulate over time. But the truth is, no matter how much we suppress it, that hurt doesn't disappear. It builds, and eventually, it demands our attention, showing up in ways we least expect it, through illness, fatigue, or even mental breakdowns.

The Parasympathetic Mind:

This is where the real healing begins, in understanding that to achieve the ultimate fix, we must first bring the mind back to a state of ease. We must allow the mind to find peace, to release the grip of worry, anger, and sadness. Only when we do that can we truly begin to heal the body. The journey of healing cannot simply be about treating the physical symptoms; it has to start with the mind. And the most powerful way to restore the balance is through the Parasympathetic Way, the calming, restorative force that allows us to return to a state of relaxation, peace, and regeneration.

The Parasympathetic Nervous System is the body's natural state of healing. It's the "rest and digest" mode, where the body can repair itself, rebuild its energy, and restore balance. It's the opposite of the stress response, the "fight or flight," and it's here that true healing happens. When the mind is calm, when we consciously activate this healing response, we give the body the space it needs to recover. The Parasympathetic Mind embraces stillness, peace, and mindfulness. It's a mind that understands the importance of self-care, of letting go, of trusting that everything is unfolding as it should.

It's in this place of quiet and calm that healing begins, not just physically, but emotionally and spiritually as well. When we give our mind the space to rest, to heal, to find ease, the body naturally follows. The disease that once seemed so overwhelming starts to fade as the body remembers how to heal itself.

This Parasympathetic Mind is not just a state we strive for in times of illness, but a way of life. It's about choosing peace over panic, stillness over stress, trust over fear. It's a constant reminder that we don't have to be at war with ourselves or with our bodies. Healing is not a battle. It's a journey of returning to the natural state of balance that our bodies and minds are meant to experience. And in that state of peace, we find the ultimate fix, one that is whole, lasting, and deeply healing.

CHAPTER 2

PURPOSE OF LIFE

This question, "What is the actual purpose of life?" has stirred deep emotions. It's a question that, once posed, forces us to look inward and confront the very essence of our existence. The purpose of life is not merely about achieving success, acquiring wealth, or accumulating possessions. The true purpose is far more profound. It is about resolving the karmic exchanges we have carried with us from past lives, and ultimately, seeking liberation, or Moksha.

The Web of Karmic Relationships:

Life, as we have come to understand, is a journey, a journey that spans many lifetimes. We come into this world not by chance, but as part of an ongoing cycle of birth, death, and rebirth. And as we move through this cycle, we encounter people, some who will remain close to us throughout this life, and others whom we meet only briefly. But here's the deeper truth: Every person we meet, whether family or stranger, has already crossed our path in some previous life. We are all bound by a web of karmic relationships, and the connections we share are not random, but a reflection of unfinished business from the past.

In this life, we interact with two sets of people: those who are closest to us, our parents, siblings, family, friends, and colleagues—and those we meet only briefly. And it's with those closest to us that the most intense and sometimes painful karmic exchanges occur. These are the relationships where negative karmic patterns often run deepest. The love, the hurt, the disagreements, the misunderstandings, it's all part of the unfinished business we are meant to resolve. And in these relationships, we have the power to choose. We can either continue feeding the negative energy with more anger, resentment, or blame, or we can choose to transform those interactions by responding with compassion, understanding, and forgiveness.

It reminds us that life is not about avoiding conflict or seeking comfort, but about consciously engaging with those around us in a way that heals, not hurts. Every interaction is an opportunity to resolve old karmic debts. And it is in this process of transformation, of choosing love over anger, understanding over judgment, that we can begin to free ourselves from the cycle of birth and death.

Moksha: The Ultimate Freedom

The truth is, until we clear these karmic exchanges, we will continue to be bound by them. We will continue to meet the same souls, face the same challenges, and experience the same pain. But when we start making conscious choices to resolve these exchanges, when we begin to break the cycle of negativity and choose peace, compassion, and love, only then can we truly begin to move towards liberation, or Moksha. Moksha is not an abstract concept; it is the state of being free from the karmic entanglements that bind us to this world. It is the freedom to no longer be part of the cycle of birth and death, but to reside in the eternal peace of Param Dham, the realm of the Divine.

This, I believe, is the true purpose of life. Life is not just about living, but about resolving, healing, and transcending. Every interaction, every relationship, every challenge we face is an opportunity to clear our karmic debts, to transform negative exchanges into positive ones, and to move closer to the ultimate goal: Moksha.

And yet, this journey begins with understanding who we truly are. It requires us to look beyond our physical existence, to recognize that we are not just the body or the mind, but the soul, an eternal being on a journey of growth, healing, and transformation. This knowledge has become a guiding light for me, a source of strength and understanding. It's a reminder that every moment is sacred, every interaction meaningful, and every challenge an opportunity for growth. By choosing to transform negative karmic exchanges into positive ones, we not only heal ourselves but also contribute to the healing of the world around us. And in doing so, we move one step closer to fulfilling the true purpose of life: to find freedom, to find peace, and to return home to the Divine.

Human Being:

So, what is the way to the ultimate fix? What is the path that leads to true healing, to a life of well-being and longevity? The answer lies in understanding who we truly are. When we understand the term "Human Being," we begin to see that the solution lies not just in treating the body, but in healing the soul. The word Human comes from the Latin Humus, meaning soil or earth. It reminds us that our body, the vessel we inhabit, is made of the very earth. But the being—the essence, the spirit, the soul, is far beyond the physical form. The being is the seed of life, the core of who we are, the energy that sustains and animates the body.

When we understand the interconnectedness of these two elements, our human body and our divine being, we realize something extraordinary: if our being is in alignment, our lives will naturally follow. If the essence of who we are is peaceful, balanced, and whole, then the way we live, our actions, our relationships, and our choices, will reflect that inner harmony. The path to true health and healing begins not with medications or treatments alone, but with the deep work of tending to our soul, understanding our inner nature, and cultivating a state of ease and peace within.

It's heartbreaking to think about how many people are living with chronic illness, not just in their bodies, but in their hearts and minds. How many of us are carrying burdens, unresolved emotions, and stress that block the natural flow of healing within us? When we don't attend to the health of our soul, when we don't address the emotional and spiritual wounds, the body becomes a mirror of that inner disharmony. And this is where we need to shift our focus, toward healing the Being, not just the body.

The *Ultimate Fix* is about bringing our being back into alignment, into a state of peace and balance. It's about addressing the root causes of stress, fear, and negativity that plague our minds and relationships. It's about choosing to live with awareness, with compassion, with forgiveness, and with love. Only then, when the Being is healed, can the body begin to restore itself. The human experience is a journey of remembering who we truly are, of reconnecting with the divine essence within us, and allowing that essence to guide our way of living.

The Being, the soul, the energy, the Prana, is the very essence of who we are. It is the point of light, the spark of life that runs the human body, infusing it with vitality, purpose, and direction.

The Power of Thought Energy:

What struck me most is the understanding that thought itself is energy. The thoughts we think, the beliefs we hold, the emotions we feel, they all hold a certain vibration, a certain frequency. And it is this energy that shapes the state of our body. When we realize that the mind is the driving force behind everything in our physical world, it becomes clear how powerful the connection between mind and body truly is. If the mind is strong, filled with positivity, resilience, and peace, the body follows suit. It thrives. It is free from illness, free from the burdens of chronic disease. But if the mind is weak, if it is filled with negativity, fear, stress, and unresolved emotions, the body reflects that weakness. It becomes susceptible to disease, fatigue, and imbalance.

The more we strengthen our mind, our thoughts, our attitudes, our beliefs, the more resilient we become in the face of life's challenges. We can build immunity not only to the physical ailments but also to the mental struggles that try to hold us back.

We must examine our chronic ailments with compassion and curiosity. What are they trying to teach us? Are they a reflection of the internal struggles we've been carrying for years? Are they calling our attention to something in our mind that needs healing? This deeper examination of ourselves is not about blame or guilt, but about understanding. It's about realizing that our body is speaking to us, asking us to reconnect with our soul, with our inner energy, with the power of our thoughts.

Transformation through Awareness:

And this is the most powerful part of the journey: realizing that we have the ability to change the course of our health by changing the way we think. If we focus on strengthening our mind, on nourishing it with love, positivity, and peace, we can shift the energy that runs through the mind, for the mind and body are not two separate entities, but two sides of the same coin. When we care for the mind, we care for the body. When we nurture our thoughts, we nurture our health. The ultimate resilience comes from within, from the strength of the mind, from the clarity and peace of the soul. It's in that space that healing begins, and it is from there that we can truly become disease-free, strong, and whole.

Who Am I?

Let's have an understanding of who we truly are, beyond the labels, beyond the body, and beyond the roles we play in life. We are not our bodies, not the roles we carry, and not the names we've been given. We are, in essence, the soul, the point of light, the energy, the Prana that animates the body.

For so long, I've identified with the external aspects of life, my body, my face, the labels I've acquired: daughter, mother, friend, colleague, entrepreneur. I've attached so much of my sense of self to these roles and identities. But when I take a step back and truly reflect, I realize that these labels are just the things this body has acquired, not who I truly am. I am the being within, the light that cannot be seen by the physical eyes but can only be felt with the heart.

The Illusion of Identity:

It's a humbling realization. The body is a vessel, a temporary form, and the labels are merely the roles it plays during this lifetime. But the I, the essence of who I am, is far greater. I am not bound by my appearance, age, gender, or role. I am the soul, the energy that transcends all these forms. And when I look in the mirror, I see only the body, the temporary vessel that holds the true I. The moment I say, "I am beautiful," I am speaking not of the body, but of the essence, the soul that radiates from within, the inner light that shines regardless of what the body looks like.

This insight has made me question the way I've lived my life until now. I've spent so much time focusing on the external, on achieving, on fulfilling roles, and on maintaining the body. But the truth is, none of these things can define who I truly am. The body is a tool that allows the soul to express itself in this world. It is the soul, the being, that carries the true essence of beauty, strength, and resilience.

In this journey of self-discovery, we must not only tend to the body but also nurture the soul. When we begin to meditate, when we peel away the layers of identity and reach the point of stillness, we can experience a state of bliss, of pure peace. In this stillness, we find our true self, the soul, the being that is not affected by time, space, or circumstance. It is a realization that brings freedom, that brings clarity, and that brings healing, for when we know who we truly are, we can heal at the deepest level.

So, who am I? I am not my body, I am not my face, and I am not my roles. I am the point of light, the eternal soul that shines through this body. When I remember this truth, I stop identifying with the limitations of the body and start embracing the limitless nature of the being within. This understanding is not just transformative; it is liberating. It gives me the strength to heal, to grow, and to live with purpose, knowing that I am the soul, the energy, the essence of life itself. And when I heal my soul, my body, too, will heal.

Neti—Neti: The Path of Negation to Realization:

This teaching, *Neti Neti,* "not this, not that", holds a profound truth that touches the very essence of our existence. It invites us to look deeper, to peel away the layers of identity that we so easily cling to, and to discover what lies at the core of our being. The more I reflect on it, the more I realize how deeply attached we become to our physical form, to our roles, and to the fleeting experiences of life. In this practice of Neti Neti, we are encouraged to negate everything that we perceive through our senses, for these perceptions are merely illusions. When I look at my hand, I see it, but I am not the hand. When I see my body in the mirror, I may say, "I am beautiful," but in that moment, I've forgotten the truth. I have identified myself with the body, with the temporary form that is not the essence of who I truly am. This body is a costume, something that I have temporarily acquired, but I am not the body.

What is truly humbling is the realization that the emotions we create, happiness, sadness, anger, hurt, are also not our true nature. They are responses to the roles we have assumed, to the layers we have put on. When someone praises me, I feel joy; when I am criticized, I feel hurt. But in both cases, I am reacting from the ego, the ego that is attached to the roles I have taken on. The true "I" is not affected by praise or criticism. It simply is. It is stillness. It is peace. It is love. The true "I" exists beyond all these fluctuations.

Peeling Away the Layers of Identity:

The layers we accumulate, the body, the roles, the identities, are just that: just layers. And in meditation, we begin to remove these layers, one by one, until we reach the core of our being. In the process, we learn that the true "I" is not something that we can touch or see with our physical senses. It is not defined by anything external. It is pure stillness, untouched by the world's chaos and distractions. It is the energy, the soul, the point of light that shines within, beyond all the temporary roles we play.

From Neti – Neti to Iti – Iti:

And yet, paradoxically, as we let go of all the attachments, we realize that in this stillness, we become everything. We are not just one thing, but all things. Neti – Neti leads to Iti – Iti. "Not this" leads to "this," and in the end, we realize that we are not the body, but we are in every body. We are not the thought, but we are in every thought. We are not the role, but we are in every role. It is a mystery, a paradox that cannot be fully understood by the mind, but can only be experienced in the silence of our being.

When I reach this place of stillness, of pure presence, I begin to understand that the experiences of life, the joys and sorrows, the praise and criticism, are not aimed at my true self, the soul. They are directed at the roles I have assumed. And so, I no longer feel the need to fight for anything, to defend anything, or to prove anything. The roles will come and go, but the true "I" remains unchanged, untouched by the external world.

In this state of realization, there is peace. There is freedom. There is liberation. Because when we remember who we truly are, beyond the body, beyond the roles, beyond the emotions, we experience the deep stillness of the soul. And in that stillness, we are one with everything. We are everything. We are nothing, yet we are everything. This is the great mystery, the paradox of life, and the ultimate truth that we seek to understand.

CHAPTER 3

THE NEURON

The Journey from Dependence to In-Dependence:

Most of us are mentally depleted. We feel drained, lacking the energy and strength to make lasting changes within ourselves. This depletion comes from constantly being in a state of fight or flight, responding to external stimuli, without taking the time to replenish our internal energy. But, as we begin to understand, the key to lasting change lies in becoming independent on the inside first. When we connect with our inner world, when we nurture and replenish our soul, we then find true in - dependence. **When we are in – dependant, we become independent.**

Yet, so many of us struggle to make that leap inward. We don't feel we have the strength, the motivation, or the willpower to turn within. If that's the case, we can start with the external, the body, our actions, our environment. By consciously taking care of our physical well-being, we can begin to create a ripple effect that gradually leads us back to our center.

This is where the Parasympathetic Nervous System comes in. Understanding this system is not just about biology or science. It's about understanding the very fabric of how we are wired. The vagal effect, which is a key aspect of the Parasympathetic System, is what can help us recalibrate our energy and bring us back into balance.

The Neuron: The Messenger of Life:

The nervous system, composed of trillions of neurons, is the communication network of the body. These neurons, each transmitting electrical signals, are the messengers of life. Each thought, each emotion, is an electrical impulse traveling through our body, impacting every cell. If our thoughts are negative, those neural pathways become stronger with every repetition, creating habits that are hard to break. These thoughts shape our reality, influencing how we feel, how we act, and how we experience life.

When we are trapped in negative thinking, those pathways are constantly activated, strengthening the neural connections and creating a loop of negativity. But this is not the end of the story. If we are to change, we must create a new thought, a thought that shifts the direction of those electrical impulses. We must replace the old, worn-out messages with new, healthier ones. It's like lighting a new bulb on the highway of our mind, and with each new thought, we gradually illuminate a new path.

Creating New Pathways of Light:

The power lies within us to change our neural pathways, to shift the way we think, feel, and act. It takes effort, it takes awareness, but it is possible. The journey inward is not always easy, but it is the most rewarding journey we can take. When we begin to nurture our inner world, the outside world begins to fall into place.

So, let's start today. Let's begin with small steps, with simple actions, and move toward a life that is not just physically healthy but emotionally, mentally, and spiritually whole. The ultimate fix, the true cure, comes when we take care of both the inside and the outside. When we understand that thought is energy, and that the mind is the key to unlocking the body's potential, we realize that we are not just passive participants in life. We are the creators of our reality. And the moment we take control of our inner world, the outer world will follow.

CHAPTER 4

WHAT IS LIFE FORCE?

Life force energy is called Prana in Sanskrit, an Indian language. Life force is the energy of the soul itself, eternal, pure, and self-luminous. The body is a vessel through which the soul's energy expresses itself. The soul never dies; it simply changes forms, carrying its vibration and memory.

When we connect to this level of life force through meditation or stillness, we experience peace, clarity, and bliss, because we touch our original nature.

From Thought to Destiny:

Every thought we create is a seed, and like seeds, it grows into something far greater. It begins as a single thought, but soon that thought is accompanied by a feeling, an emotion that resonates with the heart. Over time, when that feeling resurfaces, it turns into an attitude. We begin to form perspectives about people, situations, and even ourselves based on this repeated attitude. Our thoughts, feelings, and perspectives don't just disappear; they shape our reality. This is the essence of our karma.

Karma is not just about actions. It is the accumulation of our thoughts, emotions, and attitudes that drive us to act in certain ways. These actions, repeated over time, become habits, ingraining themselves deeply into our personalities and our souls. Our actions create consequences, and these consequences, in turn, form our destiny. That is the profound truth: thoughts create destiny.

The Power of Vibration:

It's incredible how deep the connection is between our thoughts, emotions, and the energy we radiate. A single negative thought doesn't just stay inside us; it shapes our entire being, our state of mind, and even our physical health. The body reacts as if it's under attack, flooding with cortisol, tightening muscles, and slowly, without us realizing it, turning emotional pain into physical suffering.

And what's even more powerful is how this energy doesn't stop with us. Thoughts are pure energy, and energy moves. When that thought is directed at someone else, it doesn't just vanish, it travels, carrying its vibration with it. When the energy is negative, it lowers the frequency of the person it touches, subtly draining them, dimming their light, and weakening their own aura.

The Healing Frequency of Love:

It's a painful realization because it shows how connected we truly are. However, at the same time, there's something incredibly beautiful hidden within this truth: if our negative energy can deplete someone, imagine the healing power of love, kindness, and compassion. Imagine sending thoughts of peace, forgiveness, or understanding, that same connection could uplift, heal, and restore not just others but ourselves.

We are responsible for the energy we carry and share. What we send out inevitably comes back. And in that responsibility, we find our greatest power, to heal, to nurture, and to transform not just ourselves, but everyone around us.

The Earth Reflects Our Collective Energy:

This reflection is incredibly powerful. It speaks to a truth that resonates on a soul-deep level: *everything is connected.* Every relationship we nurture, every thought we carry, and every emotion we release contributes to an invisible, yet deeply felt, energy ring. Two people sharing a bond create a circle of energy that doesn't stop with them, it expands, influencing the room they're in, the home they share, and beyond. It's like a wave that keeps moving, touching spaces we can't even see but can undoubtedly feel.

When the energy between people is heavy, filled with fear, anger, or sorrow, it doesn't just stay confined. It seeps into the environment, feeding a collective vibration that stretches from our immediate surroundings to the world itself. It's heartbreaking to think that the suffering of humanity could be echoing so loudly that it stirs the very earth beneath us, manifesting as earthquakes, tsunamis, and floods. It's as if the planet is crying out, reflecting the chaos and imbalance we've projected outward.

But within this overwhelming truth lies something even more powerful: hope. If our negative thoughts can ripple through the universe, then so can love, kindness, and peace. Imagine what would happen if we all chose to heal our inner wounds, forgive ourselves and others, and cultivate compassion. That energy could shift not just the mood of a room, but the very heartbeat of the world.

Changing the universe starts within. Every loving thought, every moment of gratitude, every act of forgiveness becomes a light in the darkness. And when enough of us shine together, we don't just heal ourselves, we heal the world. Thought can impact the universe.

The Soul: The True Source of Life Force:

As we reflect on the concept of the human being, we realize that at our core, we are energy. This energy, this life force, is what defines us, what makes us who we are. We call it the Soul, the Prana, the Urja, the Life Force. It is an immortal, ever-moving energy that cannot be destroyed. This energy flows through us, through pathways known as chakras, meridians, and nadis, guiding us through life.

But here's where it becomes deeply personal: every soul, every being, is a point of light, and every point of light is imbued with the same original qualities, Love, Peace, Happiness, Purity, Power, Knowledge, and Bliss. These are the foundational qualities of the soul, the very essence of who we are before we acquire any of the labels or layers that come with our journey on this earth.

However, as we go through life, we accumulate experiences, attachments, and responses to the world around us. These become our **files**, the folders that store our acquired personality traits, our Sanskars. Some of us create files of anger, others of jealousy, insecurity, hurt, anxiety, greed, and lust. These negative emotions and reactions slowly begin to overshadow the original qualities of the soul, leaving us feeling disconnected from our true essence.

We start searching for love, peace, and happiness outside ourselves, never realizing that these qualities are already within us. We are so busy creating the opposite, anger, fear, judgment, and pride, that we forget our inherent state of bliss, love, and peace.

Ego vs. Self-Respect:

But here's the key: **when I am in my original state of being**, I am in a state of self-respect. In this state, I do not need to prove myself to anyone. I do not need to seek validation, because I know my worth. **When I shift away from my original qualities,** I enter a state of ego, where I begin to identify with the temporary layers I've accumulated rather than the eternal essence of who I am.

Healing through Awareness and Pause:

The process of reclaiming our true essence starts by being aware of these acquired traits, these layers and making the conscious choice to return to our original qualities. It's not about changing who we are, but rather about shedding the unnecessary layers that hide the light within us. It's about remembering who we truly are. Souls of love, peace, and bliss.

As we shift from ego to self-respect, from acquired traits to original qualities, we begin to experience a profound transformation. We start to heal, to align, and to reconnect with our true self. And as we do, we realize that the power to create a beautiful destiny is always within us. It's in our thoughts, our emotions, and our ability to choose the energy we put into the world.

For so long, we've been living with the acquired Sanskars, those habits, reactions, and patterns that our experiences, fears, and external influences have shaped. These acquired traits have become automatic, always ready to surface when we face certain situations. They feel familiar, but they don't always serve us. The truth is, they often distance us from the peaceful, loving, and balanced beings we truly are at our core. The original Sanskars, the true qualities of our soul, like love, peace, and compassion have been dormant for too long.

To change, we need to consciously return to these original Sanskars. We need to remember the essence of who we truly are and begin using those qualities more with the same discipline we once gave to our acquired traits. But here's the challenge: it takes mindfulness and patience. It's not something that happens overnight. Just like any skill, it requires practice. The way we can start is by increasing the gap between the stimulus, what happens to us or around us, and our response.

When we react impulsively, it's like a reflex; we've done it so many times that it has become automated. But when we take a step back, pause, and let ourselves breathe before responding, we give ourselves the space to connect with our true self, our soul's energy. It's in that space that we can make a conscious choice to act from love, peace, and understanding, instead of reacting out of anger, frustration, or fear.

Think of it like this: imagine injuring your right hand. At first, you avoid using it because it hurts. You start using your left hand more, even though it feels awkward at first. But with time and patience, you get used to it. Eventually, your right hand heals, but you can't go back to using it as you did before without some care and gradual practice. It's the same with our behavior. When we choose to shift back to our original qualities, it may feel uncomfortable at first. There may be moments where we feel the pull of old habits, but the more we practice using our true Sanskars, love, kindness, peace, the more natural it becomes.

Over time, these original qualities will feel like home. They will become the most comfortable, natural way of being. They will bring us peace and ease. And when we start responding instead of reacting, we allow ourselves to reconnect with the energy of our soul. Every act of kindness, every moment of peace, every choice to act with love strengthens this new way of being.

Resilience Born of Alignment:

It's not always easy, but it is worth it. The more we consciously choose to act from our original essence, the more we heal. And the more we heal, the more we create a life of balance, love, and true inner strength. Just like the hand that heals with care, your soul will bloom again with patience and practice. Keep going, step by step, thought by thought, until your true self is not just a memory, but your living reality.

We can embody a profound resilience, a quiet, steady strength that reveals itself in countless ways. From the willingness to nurture others without expectation, to the courage to face life's inevitable upheavals, we can carry a power that often goes unspoken but never goes unfelt.

When we have clarity of our roles, there are no questions. The mind is creating an accepting energy. It's not creating rejection. But today's generation has started asking questions. This is rejection energy that is created because of dissatisfaction, giving rise to a feeling of lack.

- **Givers at Heart:** When we give selflessly, we tap into an inner wellspring of power and compassion. This act of giving isn't about losing something; it's about expanding the heart. It's in these moments of pure generosity, caring for a child, offering emotional support, or sharing a simple gesture of kindness, that we discover just how boundless our capacity to love can be.
- **Clarity of Purpose**: In generations past, roles were often more defined. While that sometimes limited choices, it also brought a certain clarity: responsibilities were understood, and acceptance came more naturally. Today, as our roles broaden and evolve, the challenge is to maintain that clarity amid new possibilities, ensuring that any question of "Why me?" transforms into "Because I can."

- **Multitasking and Endurance:** Whether juggling work, family, personal growth, or all three at once, we have shown an extraordinary ability to adapt and thrive. The sheer intensity of childbirth alone stands as a testament to how deeply women endure and how profoundly they can transform pain into love and new beginnings.
- **Mindset and Energy:** When we ask, "Why only me?" we sometimes feed a sense of lack. But focusing on what we do we do have, the love, the skills, the courage, we can shift our energy from feeling rejected to feeling empowered. By choosing to view each challenge as an opportunity for growth, we can embrace a mindset of abundance rather than deficiency.
- **Body and Beyond:** In a world that often spotlights appearances, it's easy to become "body conscious" and lose sight of the deeper, intangible qualities that make us radiant: our wisdom, compassion, resilience, and determination. Real beauty shines brightest when we recognize our own worth—body, mind, and spirit.

Thought:

The Ripple Effect of Thought:

Life isn't just about what we do or how we live; it's deeply rooted in the choices we make in every moment, in the thoughts we create, and in the way those thoughts ripple out through our words, actions, and interactions. Think about it: when we feel happy, it's because we've chosen to create a positive, elevated thought. That thought brings energy, vitality, and a sense of connection with the world around us. But when we're sad, it's because our mind has created a negative thought, and suddenly, we feel drained and powerless. This shows us that thought is not just something we experience, it's energy itself.

Energy cannot be contained or stopped. It flows, continuously moving, shifting, and transforming everything it touches. Every moment is a passing scene, an opportunity for us to choose our thoughts. When we don't react to life, when we let go of expectations, we remain at peace. But when things don't go the way we imagined, when our desires are unmet, that's when pain emerges. The pain comes not from the situation itself, but from our attachment to the way we wanted it to be, the image we had created of how things or people *should* be.

The Root of Suffering: Attachment and Expectation

That's the root of our suffering is attachment. When we attach ourselves to an image, a person, or an outcome, we are constantly living in fear of losing it. And with that fear comes anger, frustration, hurt, and grief. But if we can realize that our thoughts are energy, we can begin to understand how our thoughts impact everything in our lives, from our relationships to our health, our atmosphere, and even our destiny. Realization is seeing things through our **REAL EYES.**

The Alchemy of Energy: Transforming Reaction into Response:

When we create a thought, it first affects us. If we hold onto negative thoughts, we absorb that negative energy within ourselves. If someone shouts at us, for instance, we might absorb their anger and internalize it as hurt. Alternatively, we might reflect that anger back, but the cycle of negativity continues. However, the true power lies in transforming that energy. When we choose to understand instead of react, when we choose peace over conflict, we can transform that energy into something positive. In doing so, we preserve our inner peace, and we change not just the energy in the room, but the entire dynamic.

Seeds of Destiny: Thoughts, Actions, and Sanskars:

What we create, we first experience ourselves. The energy we send out returns to us, shaping our relationships, our health, our surroundings, and our lives. Every thought carries the potential to affect us deeply, how we feel, how we act, how we relate to others, and ultimately, how we experience life. Our thoughts are the seeds we plant, and they grow into our experiences. Over time, they form our habits, our personality traits, our very essence.

That's why it's so important to be mindful of the energy we create. We can choose what we think, what we feel, and how we act. Each thought has the power to shape our destiny. Every feeling is an opportunity to decide how we want to respond. It's through our actions, our karma, that we build our personality, our Sanskars, and our future. And with every action, we leave an imprint on our soul, a memory of what we have experienced. These memories, these impressions, shape who we are becoming.

So, when we learn to choose our thoughts wisely, to transform negative energy, to create positivity in our minds and hearts, we begin to transform our lives. We understand that we are not just reacting to life, we are the creators of our own reality. We become conscious of the energy we put into the world, knowing that it will return to us in ways we can't even imagine.

This is the power of our thoughts. This is the power of our energy. And this is how we shape the life we want to live.

The Inner Trinity: Mind, Intellect, and Sanskar:

The life force is one energy playing different roles – Mind thinks, Intellect analyzes, Karma comes into action, and repeated Karma forms our Sanskar.

It's incredible how our soul's workings mirror our physical brain's processes. Our brain, which forms a critical part of the Central Nervous System, is designed to receive, process, and respond to stimuli, and in much the same way, the soul functions through a profound and harmonious interplay between the mind, intellect, and sanskars.

1. **Sensing and Perceiving** – Just as our brain receives input from our sense organs: eyes, ears, nose, tongue, and skin, the mind senses the world through thoughts and emotions. The mind first reacts to external stimuli, creating a thought or feeling in response to what we experience. Every moment, our mind is actively sensing what's happening in our world, processing these sensations to create our internal reality.

2. **Transmitting the Information** – The nervous system transmits information throughout the body, just as the mind sends out the thoughts that shape our responses. These thoughts move quickly, lighting up neural pathways and connecting us to the world around us. The speed with which we process our experiences

depends on the strength of these pathways, the consistency of the thoughts we choose, and how they flow through our consciousness.

3. **Processing the Information** – The brain processes the information it receives to understand the world, make sense of it, and make decisions. Similarly, our intellect plays a key role in analyzing the thoughts and emotions the mind creates. It's the intellect that weighs the information, processes it, and helps us arrive at a decision, a response to the situation that feels aligned with our values, our truth, and our highest potential.
4. Producing a Motor Response – And just like the brain sends signals to the body to initiate movement, our sanskars, the deep-seated impressions we've accumulated, drive our actions. Our past experiences, learned behaviors, and ingrained beliefs are stored in our sanskars. They become automatic, triggering certain behaviors when specific circumstances arise. These repeated actions, like habits, form the patterns of our lives.

The fascinating part is how these functions are not separate, they are interconnected. The mind, intellect, and sanskars work together, just like our brain's various functions work in synchrony. When we consciously choose to awaken and transform our thoughts, when we align our intellect with wisdom, and when we consciously rewrite our sanskars, we begin to shift the course of our lives.

Rewiring the Soul: Conscious Transformation:

We have the power to rewire ourselves. Just like the brain can form new neural pathways, we can form new patterns of thinking, feeling, and acting. It requires conscious effort, patience, and discipline, but the power lies in understanding that the energy that flows through us, in the form of thought and action, shapes our entire existence.

So, just as the brain governs and responds to the physical world, our soul governs and responds to the spiritual, mental, and emotional world. By taking charge of our inner energy, the thoughts we think, the way we process information, and the actions we take, we can create a life that is aligned with our highest self, a life filled with peace, love, and fulfillment. The journey is within, and it starts with understanding the power of our inner faculties and using them consciously to craft a life we truly desire.

The Flow of Energy: From Harmony to Blockage:

This metaphor is deeply powerful, it captures the very essence of how energy moves through us and what happens when that flow is disrupted. Just like electricity flowing through a wire, our energy, our thoughts, emotions, and life force, needs to move freely to keep us balanced and alive.

But when that flow gets stuck, even for a moment, there's a **buzzing**, an unsettling hum that echoes within us. It's that first sign of tension, irritation, or unease, subtle, but impossible to ignore. If we can release it, the energy flows again, and peace returns. But if we hold on, if fear, hurt, or frustration keeps that energy trapped, it begins to build.

The ***sparks*** come next. They're the moments when emotions escape through sharp words, frustration, or anger that bursts out unexpectedly. And if we continue to carry that blockage, if the pain lingers without release, it ignites a ***fire***, an overwhelming fury that consumes our clarity, peace, and joy. The energy that once gave us life now threatens to burn us from within.

But when the hurt is held in for too long, the *fire* ignites. The anger grows beyond what we can contain, blazing out of proportion. It consumes peace, compassion, and clarity, leaving behind regret and exhaustion. And the most painful part? When that fire burns too long, it doesn't just hurt our spirit, it begins to harm our body. The very nerves carrying our thoughts can carry the weight of that pain into our organs, manifesting as illness, as if our body is crying out for release, for healing.

Healing the Current: Restoring the Flow through Forgiveness and Love:

But the beauty in this truth is that we *can* clear the flow. We have the power to pause, breathe, release, and allow healing energy to move freely again. Just like fixing a broken wire restores the current, forgiveness, love, and understanding repair the soul. This isn't just about avoiding pain, it's about learning to let energy flow with compassion and grace so we can keep shining without burning out.

MIND:

The Wandering Mind: Lost Between Past and Future:

It's truly eye-opening to realize that whenever we use our minds, we often become trapped in a cycle of thought that takes us either backward into the past or forward into the future. The past, filled with memories, regrets, and perhaps unresolved pain, constantly pulls us back into a space of reflection. The future, with its uncertainties, desires, and worries, leads us into anticipation and often anxiety. Neither is within our control, yet we spend so much of our mental energy chasing after things that are either long gone or yet to come.

Default Mode Network:

The Default Mode Network, this wandering state of mind, is not a place of peace. In fact, it's often a place of restlessness, anxiety, and dissatisfaction. It's when we're not fully grounded in the present, not fully engaged with the reality before us, that we lose touch with our inner peace. A wandering mind, constantly shifting between the past and the future, creates more problems than solutions. It's as if we're chasing something that isn't there, draining our energy without even realizing it.

And this, unfortunately, becomes our default mode, a state of problem-focused thinking. We may think we're problem-solving, but the truth is, we're just creating more mental clutter, more emotional weight, more tension. We become entangled in what "was" and what "might be," neglecting the incredible gift of the "now." It's so easy to forget that the present moment is the only one we truly have. It's in the here and now that we can find peace, clarity, and strength.

This wandering mind, full of distractions and endless thoughts, robs us of our ability to experience life as it is, in its full beauty. But what if we chose differently? What if we could gently bring ourselves back to the present moment, time and again, with love and compassion? What if we could stop chasing what has already passed or what hasn't yet come, and simply embrace the peace and stillness that exist in the now?

The Gift of Presence: Returning to the Now:

It's not about suppressing the thoughts or avoiding the past or future, but about realizing that our power lies in the present. It's about learning to quiet the wandering mind, to reconnect with the energy of the moment, and to let go of the heavy burden of constant mental noise. When we do this, we begin to notice that the problems start to fade away, and instead, we begin to create solutions, peace, and a sense of well-being from within.

In the end, the solution isn't about fixing the past or worrying about the future, it's about learning to master our minds, to be here now, and to find the incredible power and peace that exist in this very moment.

INTELLECT:

The Present Moment: Gateway to Clarity:

It's amazing how much power the present moment holds. When I choose to be fully present, without the weight of past regrets or future worries, I tap into a state of deep clarity and peace. In these moments, I am not distracted by what's outside of me or by what has yet to come; I am simply here, engaged with the experience of the moment. This is where true happiness lies, when I am fully immersed in whatever I am doing, without the noise of constant analysis or the pressure of solving everything in an instant.

The Guiding Force Within:

But what I've come to understand is that happiness doesn't just appear by accident; it requires effort and intention. Our intellect, which is so precise, needs to be guided with clarity. When I find myself in a situation where my usual reaction isn't working, like shouting or getting angry, I must step back and make a conscious decision to change. I must tell my intellect, "Instead of reacting with anger, I will remain calm because I know that reacting will only harm my peace." The intellect listens to these instructions, but it needs clear direction to act. It needs clear instructions.

The Art of Visualization:

The key to making these changes in my life, to shifting the way I react and think, is to strengthen my intellect. And one of the most powerful ways to do this is through visualization. When I take the time to visualize positive outcomes or behavior changes, I am setting a new direction for my mind. It's like training my mind to follow a new path. Instead of just thinking about a situation, I create a vivid mental picture of how I want to respond or what I want to feel. The more I do this, the more natural it becomes.

Visualization doesn't just stay in the mind, it engages my senses. When I use my eyes to see, my ears to hear, my hands to feel, my words to speak, and even my sense of smell to experience something, I am creating a full, rich experience. These experiences get recorded in my memory, becoming the foundation for new ways of thinking and acting. As these new impressions settle into my mind, they replace old, reactive patterns. And gradually, I begin to feel more focused, more peaceful, and more in control.

The Focused Mind: A Pathway to Happiness:

The beautiful truth is that when I am truly focused, fully engaged in the present moment, I am able to bring happiness into my life. It's not about waiting for happiness to find me; it's about choosing to create it with every thought, action, and choice. By visualizing positive outcomes, directing my intellect, and embracing the present moment, I am cultivating a mind that is not just focused but deeply content and at peace.

This focused mind, one that chooses calm over chaos, clarity over confusion, is a happy mind. And I can feel that happiness radiate through every part of my life. It's a beautiful, ongoing process of learning to let go of the unnecessary, to step into the present, and to create a future that aligns with my highest purpose and peace.

By focusing on a proactive response, we take back our power. We become the ones who choose how we feel, how we act, and how we allow others to impact us. In these moments, peace is found. When we are proactive instead of reactive, we create space for ourselves to breathe, to heal, and to move forward. No more waiting for the other driver to wake up. No more crashing into others with our own unconscious reactions. We are awake. We are aware. We are in control.

And most importantly, we are at peace.

Conscious Mind and the Subconscious Mind:

How are habits formed:

An act done a number of times is called habit. Whenever we try doing any task for the first time, the mind will create two types of thoughts, one is logical thoughts and the other is emotional thoughts. It will behave like two lawyers arguing with each other. This argument continues till the intellect doesn't evaluate the debate and arrives at a decision. The intellect behaves like a judge. This decision depends on how strong the intellect is. The decision is normally based on our habits or Sanskars and the type of information we have been consuming.

The Smoking Analogy: From Thought to Pattern:

Imagine the very first time a Being created a thought of smoking a cigarette because he was anxious and undergoing stress. His mind behaves like 2 lawyers, debating. One lawyer says, this is not a good thing to do, and there are various health hazards associated with the act. The other lawyer would say, it's okay to do it once and it wouldn't cause any harm if done once.

Now if the intellect decides to smoke, and after smoking the being experiences relaxation, this experience gets recorded on our memory bank, the Hippocampus. He has just created an impression that when I am anxious and if I smoke, I feel relaxed.

Now, the next time the Being is anxious, the mind will create a thought of smoking because the impression is already stored in the memory bank. This time again, the Lawyers will argue.

If the decision is taken to smoke and the person again feels relaxed, the impression is further etched on the memory bank. A person has to do it 21 times, and the mind will keep debating.

Now, if the decision is always to smoke, then the action eventually enters an automated mode. Earlier, which was a conscious decision, went into an automated mode. Since we have repeated the same action or karma a number of times, it has now formed a habit. After this, the mind and intellect is bypassed and the person ends up smoking. This has gone into the unconscious mode. Most of our emotions have been created so many times that they have all gone into an automated way.

Hence, when a situation arises, we react immediately. Since our reaction is so quick, we feel that the other person or the situation is responsible for our reaction.

The metaphor of the mind as two lawyers arguing and the intellect as a judge is quite powerful. It highlights the importance of strengthening our intellect through conscious awareness, right knowledge, and disciplined thinking.

The example of smoking perfectly demonstrates how habits and past experiences shape our decisions. If our intellect is weak or influenced by past conditioning (Sanskars), it may lean toward the easier or more tempting choice. However, if the intellect is strong and well-nourished with positive values and knowledge, it will make wiser decisions.

The Role of Mindfulness in Reprogramming the Subconscious:

This also emphasizes the role of mindfulness in daily life. By being aware of this internal debate, we can consciously guide our intellect toward choices that align with our long-term well-being.

Our conscious state is a state of awareness but the interesting part is that most of our decisions are automatic and taken unconsciously.

Today in a day almost 90% of our actions are repeated. We are not doing anything different on any given day. This means that 90% of the time, we use our subconscious mind, and the conscious intellect is only sparingly applied.

But it's not just smoking. This is how we form habits in every aspect of our lives, whether it's reacting with anger, or withdrawing in fear, or feeling hopeless in the face of challenge. The pattern repeats and the automatic reactions take over. And what happens then? We feel stuck, as though we are bound by something we can't control, as if these reactions and habits are beyond us. But in truth, they are only reflections of past decisions, decisions that we can choose to change.

From Reaction to Creation:

We can ask ourselves today: Are we happy with these reactions? Do they serve us? Do they bring us peace? Do they bring us joy? If not, then we have the power to change them. It's hard, it's uncomfortable, and it feels like fighting against our own nature. But we can consciously choose to respond differently. The key is in breaking the cycle. If we can pause, if we can allow ourselves the space to evaluate and bring awareness to our choices, then we can start the process of creating new, empowering impressions in our mind.

The first step may feel awkward and uncertain, like fighting a battle between the old and the new, like those two lawyers arguing back and forth. But with each conscious choice, the new response begins to take root. If we keep practicing it, if we decide again and again to change the response, over time, it will become our new reality.

This is how we reshape our habits and, ultimately, our lives. It's not an overnight change, but a daily commitment to breaking free from what no longer serves us and, instead, consciously choosing a different way of being. And over time, we'll realize that we are no longer prisoners of our habits. We are the creators of them, and we can change them, one choice at a time.

So let us remember in every moment, we have the power to choose. Our actions may be automatic now, but that doesn't mean they have to remain so. The freedom is in our hands; the strength is in our hearts. The choice is always ours.

How can we change our habits?

To change any habit we need to ask ourselves:

1. Why do we need to change?
2. Do we want to change?
3. How to change?

1. Habits are acquired traits. We need to concentrate on those habits that are not working for us.

Any habit that depletes me:

affects my mind

affects my relationship

affects my health

affects my environment

Honest Self-Reflection:

Changing our habits is a journey that begins with a deep, honest reflection of ourselves. It's a process that demands vulnerability and commitment. We are creatures of habit, shaped by the routines, actions, and emotions we've lived with for so long. But the question we must first ask ourselves is: *Why do we need to change?*

It's not just about the superficial desire to change for the sake of change. It's about recognizing the toll that certain habits take on our lives. Habits that deplete us emotionally, mentally, physically, ultimately rob us of the joy, peace, and fulfillment that we deserve. These habits might feel comforting or familiar in the moment, but over time, they affect our mind, our relationships, our health, and even the energy around us. They make us feel disconnected from our true selves.

2. If the desire to change is not there, I have not started my journey. Do we really want to change? Change is hard, it's uncomfortable, and it often means stepping into the unknown. We have to ask ourselves: Am I truly ready to let go of what has become familiar, even though it no longer serves me? Change isn't just about stopping certain behaviors; it's about shifting our mindset, our perspective, and our emotional responses. It's a deep inner shift. It's about moving away from our comfort zone.

If we find ourselves justifying our reactions, blaming others, or holding on to the idea that "I'm not wrong," then we haven't truly begun our journey of change. It's not about waiting for someone else to change. It's about realizing that the power to transform ourselves lies within us. And until we embrace that responsibility, until we take ownership of our emotions, our responses, and our actions, we will remain stuck in the same cycle.

3. How do we change? This is where the true work begins. We have to be deliberate, mindful, and disciplined. It's not an overnight transformation, but a gradual process of choosing differently each day. It's about replacing those old, depleting habits with new ones that nurture us, habits that empower us, habits that align with our true selves. Every time we make a conscious choice to respond differently, we are reprogramming our minds and our hearts.

The Process of Change:

Changing a habit is like breaking free from chains that have bound us for so long. It's about reclaiming our energy, our peace, and our power. But we cannot change what we're not willing to confront. We cannot heal what we refuse to acknowledge. So, the first step is to be honest with ourselves. The next is to commit, to take that first step, no matter how small, and begin the journey toward becoming the best version of ourselves.

Reprogramming the Mind:

We all carry a history of emotional responses, a collection of reactions that have shaped who we are. Over time, we've created patterns, repeated behaviors, and responses so many times that they've become automatic. The gap between what happens to us and how we react has become so small that we often feel as though our reactions are out of our control. We blame the situation, the people, or the circumstances for how we behave. But in truth, we are reacting through the filter of our acquired personality traits, our **Sanskaras.**

But deep down, we know there is another way. When we connect to our original Sanskaras, those core qualities of love, peace, and truth, we feel a deep sense of comfort, balance, and ease. These are the responses that come from our true nature, the soul. However, because we've been so caught in the web of our acquired reactions for so long, reconnecting to our original way of being requires conscious effort. It's like waking up from a deep sleep.

The Power of the Pause:

In those moments when we pause, when we allow ourselves to feel the weight of the choice before us, we create space for the intellect to step in. It's in that pause that the magic happens. We can choose to create a new thought, a new response. But it doesn't happen automatically. It requires effort, mindfulness, and intention. The debate begins. The "lawyers" of our mind start to argue, and the intellect is once again called into action. If we choose to listen, if we choose to use that moment of pause to guide our thoughts, we can create a new response. A response that aligns with our inner peace, our truth, and our strength.

The power is in our hands. The intellect may have been quiet for too long, but it has never left us. It is still there, waiting to guide us toward the right decision. With patience, practice, and love, we can begin to strengthen it again. And with every new response, we start to form new patterns, patterns that reflect our true essence and bring us closer to the life we truly desire.

In this moment, we are invited to reconnect with who we truly are, to choose the path of conscious thought and response, and to create habits that serve us, habits that bring us back to our original self. It won't always be easy, but it will always be worth it. Every time we make a new choice, we are rewriting our story. We are becoming the person we've always meant to be.

Thoughts can be categorized into various types:

Our thoughts are the very foundation of our emotional and spiritual state. They shape our reality, guide our decisions, and influence how we interact with the world. Yet, many of us are unaware of how the type of thoughts we create can either nurture or drain us.

Negative thoughts, those that arise from jealousy, anger, anxiety, or criticism, can feel like an overwhelming weight. They consume our energy, leaving us feeling depleted, resentful, and disconnected from our true selves. The more we indulge in them, the further we drift from our inner peace. It's as if we are feeding a dark cloud that only grows heavier, blocking the light of our soul.

Necessary thoughts, those related to the daily tasks and responsibilities we must manage, are often neutral. They are neither uplifting nor depleting but exist simply to ensure the smooth flow of our day. Yet, we are often so caught up in them that we forget to pause and check in with ourselves. These thoughts become a distraction, pulling us further away from the present moment, from truly living. Sometimes necessary thoughts are followed by negative thoughts if we start to create anxiety, fear, or resentment.

Waste thoughts, those that dwell on the past or worry about the future—are perhaps the most subtle and insidious. We replay old hurts, ruminate on what could have been, or anxiously anticipate what might happen. These thoughts are like anchors, keeping us stuck in a time that no longer exists or in a future that is uncertain. And in this cycle, we lose touch with the precious moment we are living right now. It's easy to get lost in this constant loop, believing that we are powerless over our emotions or circumstances. But we are not.

Then, there are the **positive thoughts**, those that uplift and elevate our energy. When we choose thoughts that are rooted in acceptance, love, and compassion, we begin to feel a shift within. These thoughts may not be revolutionary, but they open the door to a more harmonious existence. We begin to see the goodness in others, in ourselves, and in life itself. It's in these moments that we feel lighter, more connected, and more alive.

And finally, there are the **elevated thoughts**, the highest form of thought. These are the thoughts that arise from deep within our soul, affirming our truth and connection to the universe. When we remember, "I am a pure soul," or "I am a happy soul," we are reminding ourselves of our inherent nature. These thoughts are not just words, they are the very vibration of our being. And when we send them out into the world, they return to us with the power to transform everything around us.

Yet, it's staggering to realize that 85% of our thoughts are tied to the past or the future. We live so much in "what has been" or "what might be" that we rarely take the time to fully experience "what is". It's no wonder that we often feel like we're chasing happiness, always just out of reach, never fully present in the now.

But we have the power to change this. We can choose our thoughts. We can shift our energy from negative or wasteful thinking to positive and elevated thoughts. We can make a conscious effort to reconnect with our soul's essence and remember that true happiness is not something we need to chase, but something we can create within ourselves in every moment.

The choice is ours. And when we begin to choose thoughts that uplift, that affirm our truth, and that align us with love and peace, we begin to experience the happiness we have been seeking all along. It's not found in the future, nor in the past, but in the now, in the power of our thoughts.

CHAPTER 5

RELATIONSHIP : THE UNSEEN BOND

The Silent Conversation That Shapes Our Relationships:

Our minds are constantly engaged in an ongoing conversation, an inner dialogue that shapes everything around us. This conversation, whether we realize it or not, deeply influences the quality of our relationships. Often, we focus so much on our words and actions, on what we say or do, that we forget the most profound impact comes from how we think about others and how they, in turn, think about us.

At the heart of any relationship is not just what we express outwardly, but the unspoken thoughts that reside in our minds. When we think kindly, with empathy and understanding, we naturally express that warmth in our words and actions. But when our thoughts are clouded by judgment, assumptions, or negativity, those feelings seep into our interactions, creating distance, misunderstanding, or even conflict.

The Energy Behind Our Words:

Think about it: how many times have we felt misunderstood, even when we said all the "right" things? The words may have been correct, but the energy behind them, the thoughts we carried with us, spoke louder. Our thoughts create a silent current that flows through every interaction, and if our thoughts about others are filled with resentment, frustration, or even subtle criticism, that energy permeates our relationships. People can feel it, even if it's unspoken. **DO NOT RAISE YOUR VOICE, RAISE YOUR WORDS.**

In the same way, how we imagine others perceive us can affect how we show up in relationships. If I believe that others see me as unworthy or flawed, I may pull back, guard my heart, or be defensive, even if that's not their perception at all. On the other hand, when I feel loved, respected, and valued by others, when I believe they think well of me, I naturally open up and connect on a deeper level.

This mutual exchange of thoughts, how we think of others and how others think of us, creates the foundation for every relationship. The deeper our understanding of this, the more intentional we become with our thoughts. The more we practice kindness, compassion, and appreciation in our inner dialogue, the more these qualities reflect in the relationships we build.

True connection comes not only from our actions but from the space we create with our thoughts. And in that space, we allow love, trust, and understanding to flow freely. Relationships become a mirror of the conversations we have within ourselves. When we think with love and acceptance, we invite those same energies into our lives. And when we think critically or harshly, we unintentionally push those we care about away.

So, the next time you find yourself questioning why a relationship feels strained, pause and reflect on the inner conversation you are having. What are you thinking about the other person? And more importantly, what are you thinking about yourself? This awareness holds the key to transforming our relationships and creating connections that are built on the foundation of love, trust, and mutual respect.

It's heartbreaking, isn't it? When we speak words that sound kind and gentle, even though the energy behind those words is filled with negativity, dissatisfaction, or even resentment. On the surface, everything may seem fine, smiles, pleasantries, the right words at the right time. But beneath it all, there is a deeper truth: energy always speaks louder than words.

The Illusion of Separation:

When we're caught in a cycle of negative thinking, even though our actions may seem perfect, the energy we carry becomes the true message. The person on the other side might not consciously know what's happening, but they can feel the tension, the undercurrent of unhappiness, or the unspoken discontent. This energy transfers, whether we acknowledge it or not, and it becomes the silent force that shapes our relationships. It's like two people standing in the same room, yet feeling miles apart, because one absorbs negative energy while the other deflects it. We may be physically present, but emotionally we are worlds away.

Think about the times when we've been on the receiving end of such energy. We may have heard all the right words, but something felt off, like a heaviness that lingered in the air. Those moments are reminders that our energy has a profound effect on the quality of our connections. It's not just what we say but how we feel, think, and transmit those unspoken emotions to the people around us.

And here's the painful truth: we often find ourselves seeking the soul's original qualities: love, peace, joy, and happiness, from others, thinking they hold the key to our fulfillment. But in doing so, we forget that these qualities already reside within us. The more we look to others to fill the emptiness we feel inside, the more we continue to miss the point. The only way to experience true connection, true love, and true peace is by first reconnecting to the original essence of who we are.

Seeking from Others What Already Resides Within:

We often seek happiness from the people around us, but they, too, are looking for it from us. And when we're stuck in negative emotions or dissatisfaction, we unintentionally block the flow of these soul qualities, not just for ourselves, but for the others we encounter. Relationships can only thrive when we recognize that the energy we carry is what shapes them.

When we begin to focus on our own internal energy, when we nurture the qualities of love, acceptance, and peace within ourselves, we stop expecting others to "give" us these things. Instead, we create a space where these energies flow naturally, allowing others to do the same. The more we cultivate this positive energy within, the more we radiate it outward, and the more we draw those same soul qualities into our relationships.

Breaking the Cycle of Blame:

It's so easy, isn't it? To get caught in the cycle of blaming others for our pain, our stress, our anger, and our unfulfilled desires. We hold onto the belief that these emotions are natural, that it's okay to feel hurt, frustrated, or resentful when things don't go the way we expect. But what if we took a step back and saw things differently?

What if we acknowledged that at the core of all these emotions, lies a deep need for understanding and connection, but instead of looking outward for answers, we looked within? How often do we truly pause to ask ourselves, Why am I feeling this way? Instead, we quickly point fingers, expecting someone else to change, to make things right for us. But in doing so, we only trap ourselves in more pain, because blame only intensifies the suffering.

Relationships as Mirrors of Our Inner State:

When we blame others, we hand over our power, our peace, and our happiness to them. We let them define how we feel. And in that moment, we forget that others do not dictate our emotions, they are born within us. Yes, relationships are a dance between two souls, but the energy we bring to the table is what ultimately defines them. If we are coming from a place of hurt, of resentment, we are setting the tone for the entire connection.

Just as negative energy flows from one person to another, so can positive energy. If we can let go of blame, take responsibility for how we feel, and shift our focus to what we can bring to the relationship, we can create a different kind of flow, one of love, understanding, and acceptance. This isn't about ignoring our emotions or pretending everything is okay. It's about acknowledging our feelings, but also realizing that we have the power to change the energy we bring into the room.

The Choice That Changes Everything:

When we make the choice to act from a place of inner peace, to let go of blame, and to embrace our own responsibility for our happiness, we start to shift the energy within us. And when we do that, we can begin to feel a profound change in our relationships. The pain, the anger, the resentment, these things lose their grip on us because we no longer let them dictate how we feel. We choose to be the source of our own energy.

The next time we feel hurt or frustrated, let's pause and remember: We are not powerless. We can choose how we respond, how we feel, and how we connect. We can choose to break the cycle of blame, and instead, we can become the positive energy that our relationships so desperately need. It all starts with us.

RESPONSIBILITY:

The Illusion of External Happiness:

For so long, we believed that our responsibilities were outward-focused. We thought that happiness would come from what we acquire, our possessions, our relationships, our achievements. We thought that if we did things for others, they would be happy, and through their happiness, we would find our own. But how often do we find ourselves disappointed when others don't meet our expectations? How often do we feel unfulfilled when the love, recognition, or respect we give isn't returned in the way we hoped?

The First Responsibility: Ourselves:

The truth is, we've been giving so much of ourselves away, expecting, needing, and wanting from others and when that doesn't happen, we become disillusioned. In doing so, we lose sight of something crucial: our first responsibility is to ourselves.

If we cannot take control of our own emotions, thoughts, and reactions, then we will never truly be able to foster harmony in our relationships. It is impossible to create peace when we are sending out turbulence from within. A disturbed mind creates more disturbance, and the result is conflict, frustration, and pain.

The Power of Inner Discipline:

Imagine for a moment: what if, instead of expecting others to make us happy, we focused on cultivating peace within ourselves first? What if we made the decision to take full responsibility for how we feel, how we react, and how we show up in the world? The energy we bring into any interaction will shape the outcome. If we are calm, centered, and at peace with ourselves, others will feel that energy. They will be more open to understanding us and listening to us. But if we come from a place of turmoil, expecting others to fix us, we will only continue to face conflict.

The Search Within:

It all starts with us. We must be disciplined with ourselves, owning our thoughts, our actions, and our reactions. Only when we truly take responsibility for our own state of mind and energy can we shift the dynamic of our relationships. We can stop searching for love, happiness, and peace outside of ourselves and instead begin to recognize that we already have all of these qualities within us. They have always been there, waiting for us to rediscover them.

Reclaiming Emotional Independence:

We are so often so focused on what others should do for us that we forget to nurture ourselves first. But when we learn to prioritize our own well-being, when we take charge of our own peace, we can offer it to the world in a way that will transform everything around us. It's time to stop searching for what we already have. It's time to be responsible for ourselves, and in doing so, we can bring harmony into all our relationships.

The mistake we've all made is that we've spent so much of our lives searching for happiness, peace, and fulfillment in the external world, never realizing that everything we long for is already within us. The truth is, happiness is not something that can be found in people, in circumstances, or in possessions, it's something that we create, experience, and radiate from within ourselves.

The Trap of Emotional Dependency:

For so long, I, like many others, depended on others for my happiness. I believed that if others treated me a certain way or if situations unfolded as I desired, then I would feel content. But in that dependency, I unknowingly created fear, the fear of losing that happiness, the fear of not receiving it when I needed it most. And in that fear, I gave away my power, believing that my emotional state was controlled by the actions of others.

But the moment I understood that true independence comes from within, everything began to shift. When I stop relying on external validation and start recognizing my own ability to create joy, peace, and love, I begin to reclaim my power. The path to independence isn't about being alone; it's about realizing that my inner world is mine to control, and I am the creator of my own experience.

Yet, I also understand that this journey requires tremendous attention and discipline. Our minds have been conditioned to blame others for how we feel, to point fingers and say, "If only this person would change, if only that situation would be different, then I would be happy." But we must take a moment to pause and realize: We are the ones creating these emotions. It's not about external circumstances. It's about how we choose to respond to them. And that requires awareness. It requires courage.

In the outside world, when we face a loss, whether it's financial, professional, or material, we take action to correct it. We are alert, focused, and proactive. But when it comes to our inner world, we often ignore the signs of emotional depletion. We continue to dwell on past hurts, hold onto grudges, and let negativity seep into our thoughts without realizing the toll it's taking on our well-being. The loss grows, quietly but steadily, because we've neglected to acknowledge it.

Awareness: The First Step to Freedom:

This is why it's so crucial to develop awareness of our inner state, to become mindful of our thoughts and feelings, and to take responsibility for how we react. When we do this, we no longer give away our peace to others. We no longer wait for the world to change to make us happy. We take control of our emotional world and create the energy that we want to radiate. In this, we not only heal ourselves but begin to attract the very things we've been searching for all along.

In this example, the husband agrees to go to the movie even though he's not interested, thinking that his actions will make his wife happy. But inside, he's carrying dissatisfaction, a quiet resentment. This is where the disconnect happens: what we do externally doesn't align with what we feel internally, and the energy we radiate becomes misaligned with the love and connection we seek. The negative thoughts we harbor, about feeling unappreciated, or expecting something in return, can poison the pure intentions we have in our actions.

When there is this misalignment, when the energy behind our actions doesn't match the purity of our intentions, conflict is inevitable. No matter how much we do for someone, if the thought behind it isn't pure, it creates an invisible tension. The heart speaks louder than the actions we take, and others can feel that dissonance, even if it's unspoken.

It's so easy to fall into the trap of blaming others for how we feel. When the husband says, "I did this for you," and uses it as a weapon in the future, he is giving his wife the power to dictate his happiness. He is surrendering control over his emotional state to someone else. And that's the pain of it, we let others dictate how we feel, and in doing so, we give away our power. We allow anger, resentment, or frustration to fester because we believe our emotions are a result of others' actions.

The True Meaning of Responsibility:

This is the essence of true responsibility. Not just fulfilling obligations, but choosing the energy I bring to every situation. If I choose peace within myself, I create peace around me. If I choose to respond with love and patience, I invite those energies into my relationships. This shift in perspective is what allows us to break the cycle of conflict and create harmony, within ourselves and with others.

The Cosmic Dance of Responsibility:

Life is a cosmic dance, a graceful, ever-evolving interplay of light and shadow, of giving and receiving. In this grand performance, balance is the rhythm that keeps us moving forward. When our children are young, our hearts swell with responsibility as we nurture, guide, and protect them through their first steps into the world. Our love is the steady beat that carries them safely through wonder and chaos alike. And as the years unfold, when our own steps begin to slow, the roles gently reverse: the very children we once cradled rise to offer care and gratitude, echoing back the kindness and support we once provided.

This beautiful cycle reminds us that responsibility is not a burden but a precious gift, one that transforms and connects generations. It is in our shared duty to love, to support, and to find balance that we truly honor the dance of life. Every act of care, every tender moment of giving and receiving, contributes to the harmony of the cosmos, weaving our lives into an eternal tapestry of compassion and grace.

In this cosmic dance, each step, whether taken by a parent or a child, is essential, and each movement carries the potential to inspire, heal, and remind us that we are all part of a magnificent, interconnected whole.

Everything in life is a cycle in which every moment flows into the next. Just as the seasons shift from the fresh bloom of spring to the quiet rest of winter, our responsibilities too move and transform. When we are young, our duties are light and filled with promise, like the first rays of the morning; as time unfolds, the roles we once held begin to evolve, and we find that the care we once gave becomes the care we receive. This cycle reminds us that nothing in life is fixed. Responsibilities shift with our needs, our growth, and our experience, inviting us to embrace each change with courage and compassion. In accepting the natural ebb and flow of duty, we learn to dance with life itself, finding beauty in transition, strength in renewal, and peace in knowing that every ending gently makes way for a new beginning.

CHAPTER 6

PARASYMPATHETIC EFFECT

The Rhythm of Life: Energy in Motion:

The nervous system is such a profound reflection of how interconnected and intricate we are as human beings. At the core of our experience, everything, our thoughts, our emotions, and even our actions, is governed by the flow of energy. That energy is carried through the neurons as the electrical impulses that form the foundation of our nervous system. These impulses are like the rhythm of our lives, constantly pulsing through our bodies, guiding us, and responding to the world around us. But what happens when this flow is blocked? When the energy cannot move freely, when there is resistance in the pathways that guide us? It's like trying to breathe when the air is thick, or trying to think clearly in a fog.

Our thoughts, our very emotions, are energy, and when this energy becomes tangled, when our neural pathways are disrupted by stress, anxiety, or negative thought patterns, we feel the impact deeply. We experience mental fatigue, emotional turmoil, and even physical discomfort. It's as if we are fighting against the natural flow of life itself. And this is where the nervous system becomes so important. It's more than just a biological structure, it's the very essence of how we interact with our world.

The Nervous System as a Bridge between Body and Soul:

The Central Nervous System (CNS) is like the command center, with the brain and spinal cord as the core of our consciousness. They hold the power to process, respond, and adapt to everything around us. But what's beautiful and often underappreciated is how the Peripheral Nervous System (PNS) extends far beyond the brain and spinal cord, spreading out like a web throughout our body. It includes the Autonomic Nervous System, which we often take for granted, yet it plays such a huge role in our well-being. The Sympathetic Nervous System (SNS) kicks in during moments of stress, preparing us to fight or flee, keeping us on edge and alert. But the Parasympathetic Nervous System (PNS), the gentle, calming force, is what we need to come back to and restore balance. It's the one that nurtures our energy, soothes our thoughts, and brings us back to a place of peace.

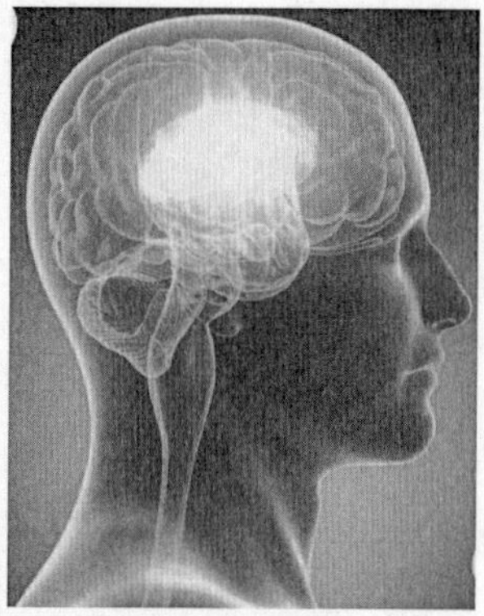

This delicate balance between the sympathetic and parasympathetic systems reminds us of the importance of creating harmony within ourselves. Just like our nervous system, our emotional and mental states need balance. When we let the stress and negativity build up, the SNS overpowers, and we feel exhausted, overwhelmed, and disconnected. But when we consciously choose to slow down, to breathe deeply, to let go of the tension, we activate our Parasympathetic Nervous System and restore the flow of energy within us.

It's a reminder that everything is interconnected. When we nurture our minds and bodies, when we take responsibility for our thoughts and emotions, we create the space for the energy to flow freely, for our neural pathways to be open and clear. In doing so, we become more attuned to ourselves, more present, and more in control of how we respond to the world around us. This is where true healing and peace lie: in the recognition that our energy, our thoughts, our body, and our spirit are all one. And when we nurture one, we heal all.

The Two Forces Within: Stress and Stillness:

The sympathetic nervous system is responsible for the body's fight-or-flight response. It reduces all the secretions in my body.

It reduces the lubrication of eyes leading to dryness, reduces salivation causing difficulty in swallowing and gag reflex, Hoarseness, reduces mucus secretion in lungs causing wheezing, reduces gastric enzymes causing acid reflux and bloating, reduces insulin secretion, Type II DM, constricts the arterial walls causing Tachycardia, Arrhythmias and Atrial Fibrillation, Erectile dysfunction, reduces intestinal motility causing constipation, reduces ovarian hormones leading to PCOD. This is known as the Acute Stress response or the Adrenaline Rush,

The parasympathetic nervous System is responsible for the Rest and Digest Body processes, breathing, and relaxing the body after stress.

It acts on glands and increases the secretions.

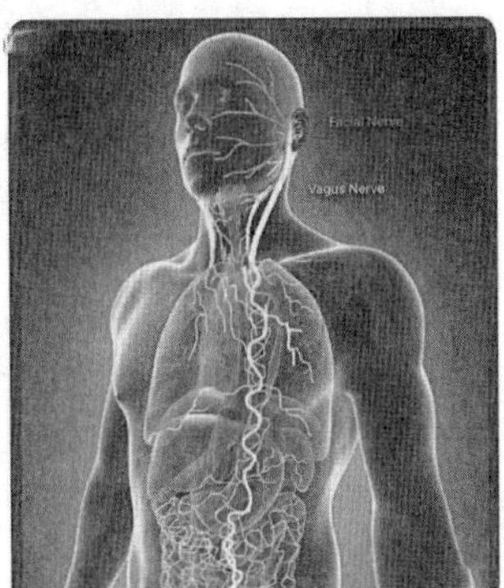

The **Vagus nerve** is the longest Parasympathetic Nerve, originating from the brainstem's medulla to the abdomen.

It's the X Cranial Nerve. Whenever we stimulate the Parasympathetic Nervous system, all our secretions increase. Parasympathetic stimulation will cause effects on various organs as follows:

Eyes - It constricts your pupils to limit how much light enters your eyes. It also makes changes that can help improve your close-up vision and cause tear production in your eyes.

Nose and Mouth - It makes glands in your mouth produce saliva, and glands in your nose produce mucus. This can be helpful with digestion and breathing

Lungs - It tightens airway muscles and ultimately reduces the amount of work your lungs do during times of rest

Heart - It lowers your heart rate and the pumping force of your heart.

Digestive tract - It increases your rate of digestion and diverts energy to help you digest food. It also tells your pancreas to make and release insulin, helping your body break down sugars into glucose a form your cells can use.

Waste Removal - It relaxes the muscles that help you control when you urinate or defecate.

Reproductive system - It manages some of your body's sexual functions, including erections in men and secreting fluids that provide lubrication during sex in women

This means that when my Parasympathetic Nervous system is activated, my body is relaxed and functioning to its optimum.

Healing Through Sleep and Stillness:

Healing happens when we are disconnected from our body in deep sleep. In those moments of rest, when we are not consciously aware of every ache or worry, our body has the chance to replenish, repair, and rejuvenate itself. It's as if, in the quiet stillness of sleep, our soul is given the space to restore its energy, free from the distractions and tensions of the waking world.

Now, imagine if we could harness that same healing power in our wakeful state. What if we could be so attuned to the present moment that we could let go of the constant chatter of the mind, the tension we hold in our bodies, and the worries that weigh us down? If we could practice the art of conscious relaxation, truly surrendering to the moment without resistance, perhaps we could access that same deep healing even when we are awake.

This is not about disengaging from life or avoiding challenges. Rather, it's about creating a balance where we are aware of our emotions, our thoughts, and our body, yet we are also able to release the need to control every detail. By doing this, we allow ourselves to heal, emotionally, mentally, and physically, just as we do in deep sleep.

Healing in a wakeful state requires a kind of trust: trust that, even in the chaos of daily life, we can find moments of stillness, and that when we pause, breathe, and truly let go, we give our bodies and souls the permission to heal. What if every breath we took, every moment of stillness, was an invitation for our mind and body to come into harmony? It's a beautiful thought, one that carries the hope of living fully in the present while still allowing the healing energy of the universe to flow through us. We have the power to heal ourselves, not only when we sleep, but whenever we consciously allow ourselves to rest in the peace of our own being.

The Illusion of the External Race:

When we buy things, achieve goals, or climb the social ladder, it often feels like we're chasing something that will finally make us feel whole. Yet, all too often, what we're truly chasing is an illusion, a fleeting sense of superiority, a momentary boost to our ego. We fall into a cycle where we push ourselves to be "better" than others, thinking that it will lead to contentment. But the truth is, there will always be someone ahead of us. And the more we compare, the more we lose sight of our own inner peace.

This race to outdo others, to constantly be on top, creates a sense of emptiness inside. No matter how much we achieve or how many things we acquire, the satisfaction we seek always feels just out of reach. It's as though we're running a marathon with no finish line, forever looking outward for something that can only be found within.

From Competition to Connection:

When we shift our focus from competing with others to connecting with ourselves, the weight of comparison begins to dissolve. True happiness is not in having more than someone else; it's in understanding that we already have everything we need to be content within ourselves. The moment we realize that the only race worth running is the one toward self-awareness, peace, and love, we can finally break free from the exhausting cycle of ego-driven pursuit.

The journey to reclaim our happiness requires courage, courage to let go of external validation, to stop measuring our worth against the opinions of others. When we embrace the truth that we are enough just as we are, we begin to experience the kind of peace that doesn't depend on being ahead or better than anyone else. The real race is within ourselves, and the reward is a life lived with authenticity and love.

The Pure Essence of the Soul:

It's deeply moving to reflect on how our true essence, as souls, is inherently pure and equal, unchanged by the external circumstances or possessions we collect along the way. In a soul-conscious state, we see everyone as equals, recognizing that within each of us lie the same innate beauty, love, and wisdom. There is no hierarchy, no need to compare ourselves or feel superior or inferior to anyone. We simply are.

The Trap of Ego and Identification:

But when we become body-conscious, something profound shifts within us. We start measuring ourselves by the things we acquire, the roles we play, and the external validation we receive. And in this state, we either elevate ourselves above others or shrink in comparison, based on what we perceive we have or lack. This is where ego creeps in, clouding our perception and distorting our connection with others. We forget that beneath our roles and possessions, we are all souls on a shared journey.

The heart-breaking part is that so many of us have been conditioned to believe this illusion. We're led to believe that our worth is tied to what we own or the status we achieve, rather than who we truly are at our core. And as a result, we create negative emotions like fear, jealousy, anger, and hurt, that not only affect our relationships with others but also block our inner growth.

These emotions, these traumas, become trapped in our minds. Over time, they form neural blockages, like scars on the heart, preventing our natural energy flow and stunting our ability to experience the peace and love that are our birthright. We become weighed down, not by the external world, but by the internal wounds we carry with us.

Healing the Neural Scars of Emotion:

Much of our suffering is self-created. Yet, within this realization lies the key to healing. When we begin to shed the layers of ego and reconnect with our soul-conscious state, we free ourselves from the chains of comparison, judgment, and fear. We create new pathways of love, forgiveness, and acceptance, both for ourselves and others.

Healing begins when we look beyond the illusions of the body and see the soul for what it truly is: pure, equal, and radiant. And as we awaken to this truth, we begin to release the trauma and negativity that have held us captive, allowing our true essence to shine through once again. The road to freedom is not through acquiring more, but through letting go of the beliefs and emotions that no longer serve us, and remembering that, at our core, we are all the same.

CHAKRAS

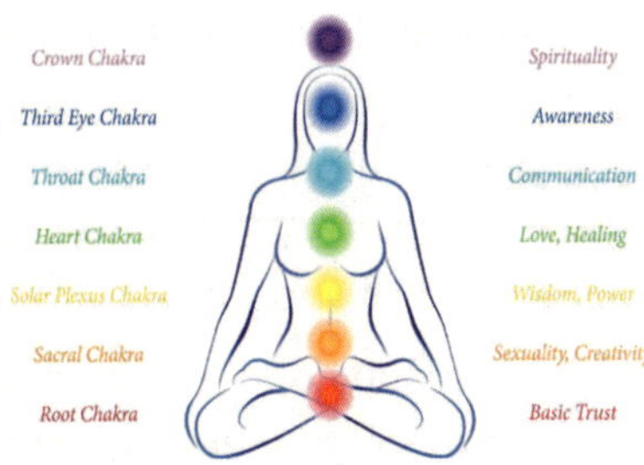

White Light — The Essence of Our Being:

The analogy of white light passing through a prism and dispersing into seven colors is so beautifully powerful. Just as the pure, untainted white light contains all the colors of the rainbow, so too does our life force energy flow through us, a source of endless potential and vitality. This life force is our essence, illuminating every part of our being, much like a radiant light touching every inch of space.

We have these sacred energy points in our body, our chakras, each one a vibrant center of power and emotion. Each chakra corresponds to different aspects of our life, body, and mind. They are like prisms, receiving the life force energy and transforming it into the colors that represent our emotional and physical states. Just as the colors of the rainbow are different but equally beautiful, so too are the energies within us.

Shadows in the Prism:

But when negative thoughts and emotions infiltrate the mind, it's as though the light within us becomes distorted. Our energy starts to disperse in unhealthy ways, and the flow of life force becomes blocked or imbalanced. Negative thoughts, like dark clouds, dim the brightness of our inner light, causing disruption in the harmony of our chakras.

This imbalance can manifest in our physical bodies in the organs connected to each chakra. When we are trapped in fear, anger, or sadness, the energy of our chakras becomes stagnant or blocked, affecting not only our emotional well-being but our physical health as well. The life force that should be flowing freely through us gets trapped, much like light that cannot pass through a prism when the glass is clouded.

The Power of Positive Intention:

The more we nurture positive, uplifting thoughts and feelings, the clearer and more vibrant our life force becomes. Our chakras align, our energy flows freely, and we experience balance, peace, and vitality.

The beauty of this understanding is that we have the power to transform our energy. We can cleanse and clear our thoughts, healing the blocks within our chakras and allowing the life force to flow through us once more in its purest form. By doing so, we restore harmony to our mind, body, and spirit, and the colors of our inner light shine brighter than ever.

Let us remember that we are not merely passive recipients of life's energy; we are the creators of the flow. Through conscious awareness and intention, we can bring healing to our chakras, align ourselves with the pure light that is always within us, and restore the vibrant, life-affirming energy that was always meant to flow freely through us.

The seven chakras are:

1. **The Root Chakra – Muladhara: Foundation of Being:**

The Sacred Ground of Existence:

The Root Chakra, or Muladhara, is the very foundation of our being. It is not just a physical center, but an emotional and spiritual anchor that connects us to the Earth and to our basic needs. When this chakra is balanced, we feel secure, stable, and deeply rooted. We trust in our ability to stand firm, no matter what life throws our way. The trust we have in our lower limbs to carry us, to support us, mirrors the trust we place in life itself. It's a deep knowing that we are safe and provided for, just as we are.

The Essence of Contentment:

When we feel contentment in our lives, it's a reflection of the Root Chakra's energy flowing freely. We realize that we don't need to constantly strive or chase after more. Everything we need is already within us and around us. There's a sense of abundance, not in terms of material wealth, but in the awareness that we have enough, enough love, enough support, enough strength to navigate life. The Root Chakra teaches us that true fulfillment comes not from what we acquire, but from what we already possess: inner peace, stability, and a sense of belonging.

Freedom from Fear and Attachment:

In this state of alignment, there's no fear, no greed, no attachment. The constant need for more fades away, and with it, the anxiety of not having enough. We become free to give and assist others, knowing that helping doesn't take away from us. It only enhances our sense of connection to the world around us. There is no fear of losing because we already feel whole, and our connection to Mother Earth is a reminder that we are supported by something much greater than ourselves.

Connection to the Earth and to All Life:

The Root Chakra is the reminder that we are not alone. We are not isolated in our struggles or our desires. The Earth beneath us is a constant source of support, grounding us and keeping us connected to our true nature. It's a soft and loving reminder that we are part of something much larger than ourselves. When we honor this, we feel the weight of our bodies grounded in trust, in safety, and in an abundant flow of energy that connects us to the present moment.

But when this chakra is disrupted, we feel the weight of fear and insecurity. We may become anxious about our safety, our finances, or our relationships. Instability can creep in, affecting our sense of belonging and our ability to trust the world. The body also speaks to us when the Root Chakra is unbalanced, manifesting as physical pain, lower back pain, fatigue, and even immune system weaknesses. These are all signals that the foundation within us needs attention.

Taking care of the physical body becomes so much more than just maintaining health. It's about nurturing a connection to the Earth. It's about honoring our bodies as the sacred vessels that allow us to walk this Earth, to feel the ground beneath our feet, and to move through life with grace and resilience.

Restoring Balance and Grounding the Energy:

One of the most beautiful ways to heal and reconnect with this energy is through grounding practices, such as yoga. Poses like the Tree Pose, Warrior Pose, or Mountain Pose help to realign and stabilize us, reminding us of our solid foundation. Each posture roots us deeper into the Earth, bringing us into harmony with our surroundings. These poses cultivate a sense of strength and inner calm, while also creating a deep awareness of the energy flowing through our bodies.

The sound of "LAM," the mantra for the Root Chakra, vibrates through us like a call to the Earth itself. It's a sound of grounding, of stability, of saying to the Universe, "I am here, I am safe, and I am whole." It echoes through our being, soothing our fears, and reminding us that we are not alone. We are supported by the Earth, by our loved ones, and by our own inner strength.

Root Chakra healing frequency is 396 Hz

2. The Sacral Chakra – Svadhisthana: The Flow of Creativity and Emotion. The Seat of Creative Energy.

The Sacral Chakra, or Svadhisthana, is our emotional center, located just below the navel. It's where our creative energy, passions, and desires flow. This chakra governs our ability to experience joy, pleasure, and intimacy, whether it's in relationships or in the simple act of creating something new, be it art, life, or experiences. It's the energy that allows us to fully embrace the beauty of the world around us and find joy in the little moments.

The Essence of Emotional Freedom:

When this chakra is balanced, we feel alive, vibrant, and connected to the world. We embrace our creativity, desire, and sexuality in a healthy, free way, knowing that these parts of ourselves are essential to our being. The Sacral Chakra enables us to express our emotions without fear or shame, and to be open to the fullness of life's pleasures.

The Shadow of Disconnection:

However, when the Sacral Chakra is blocked, it manifests in many ways. There can be a sense of numbness, a lack of emotional depth, and difficulty in connecting with others. Overindulgence may occur, where we try to fill an inner void with external pleasures, or, on the other hand, there may be a complete disconnection from desire and pleasure altogether. People may experience guilt or shame around their sexuality, leading to dysfunction or emotional repression. Physical symptoms like reproductive issues, urinary problems, or even lower back pain can signal that this energy center needs attention.

Practices like Triangle Pose, Lizard Pose, Pigeon Pose, Butterfly Pose, and Yogi Squat help open up the hips, release stored emotions, and bring a flow of energy back to this area. These poses open the body and allow energy to move freely through our sacral region, helping us reconnect to the pleasure of being alive.

And through the mantra "VAM," we vibrate the energy of this chakra, opening ourselves up to the flow of creative power, passion, and desire. This mantra reminds us to embrace life's pleasures without shame, to honor our emotional selves, and to trust the flow of life's energy.

Sacral Chakra healing frequency is 417 Hz

3. **The Solar Plexus Chakra – Manipura: The Fire of Personal Power:**

The Seat of Inner Strength:

The Solar Plexus Chakra, or Manipura, is the very core of your personal power, self-esteem, and confidence. Located in the stomach area, this chakra is the source of your willpower, your drive to take action, and your ability to influence the world around you. It's where you access your sense of control, where you tap into your inner strength and know that you are the master of your own life.

When the Solar Plexus is in balance, you feel unstoppable. You trust yourself, your decisions, and your ability to take charge of your life. You radiate confidence, not from a place of arrogance, but from the deep, unwavering belief that you have the power to create your reality. This is the energy of a true leader, someone who is capable of not only making decisions but also executing them with integrity and determination. Whether you're a businessperson, a politician, or simply someone with a vision for your life, this chakra empowers you to step into your power and positively influence others.

The Shadow of Powerlessness:

However, when this chakra is blocked or imbalanced, we begin to feel powerless. The confidence that once came naturally begins to fade, replaced with feelings of insecurity and helplessness. There may be a constant urge to control people and situations as a way of trying to compensate for the lack of control we feel within. Self-esteem plummets, and you may find yourself questioning your worth, your purpose, and your ability to succeed. Without a strong sense of self, the world can feel overwhelming and chaotic, leaving you feeling lost and without direction.

Physical and Emotional Manifestations:

A blocked Solar Plexus Chakra can also manifest in physical symptoms like digestive issues, fatigue, and emotional burnout. These are the warning signs that your energy, your "inner fire," is not burning brightly. When we lose touch with our core strength, our bodies, too, suffer the consequences.

But the beauty of the Solar Plexus Chakra is that, when balanced, it can empower you to reclaim your sense of self. Practices like Boat Pose, Triangle Pose, Plank Pose, Bow Pose, and Downward Facing Dog help activate and strengthen the core, re-establishing your connection to your own inner power. These poses are about building strength from the centre of your being, allowing energy to flow freely through your solar plexus and restore your confidence.

And through the chant of "RAM," you invoke the energy of Manipura, calling upon your inner fire to burn brightly once again. When the Solar Plexus Chakra is open and balanced, you feel empowered to act, to lead, and to make decisions that align with your highest self. You regain a sense of control, self-worth, and inner peace. You are no longer seeking validation from the outside world, because you've already found your power within. It is in this state that you can truly step into your purpose, influence others, and live with the confidence that you are the master of your life.

4. **The Heart Chakra – Anahata: The Bridge of Love and Connection:**

The Bridge Between Earth and Sky:

The heart chakra, or Anahata, truly represents the bridge between the physical and the spiritual, the self-preserving and the expansive. While the lower three chakras focus on survival, on grounding, security, and personal power, the upper three are about connection, self-expression, and spiritual transcendence. The heart chakra is where these two dimensions meet, where we find the balance between nurturing our own needs and reaching out to embrace the world around us.

The Essence of "Anahata" – The Unstruck Sound:

It's not just a chakra, it's the essence of who we are, the center of our being. The name "Anahata," meaning "unstruck," speaks to the purity of the heart's energy, untouched, unbroken, and ever-present, regardless of life's challenges.

It is in the heart chakra that we experience the transformative energy of love, not just the love for others, but the love for ourselves, for our journey, and for the very essence of life. It is the place where self-preservation shifts into self-expression, where the fear of not having enough or being enough transforms into the trust that we are all interconnected, and that our love can flow freely, unconditionally, without fear of scarcity.

The heart chakra doesn't just connect us to the people we love; it connects us to the universe. It teaches us that to give love, we must first cultivate it within. This chakra is the essence of human connection, the force that allows us to understand that we are not separate, but part of a greater whole.

When our heart chakra is open and balanced, we can stand in the middle of the emotional spectrum, strong in our own truth, but open to the truth of others. We begin to feel that we belong, not just to our families, or our circles, but to the whole of creation. It is here that we learn that love is not something we take or demand, but something we can offer freely, without conditions, without expectations, knowing that in giving, we receive.

But if this chakra is blocked, we may struggle with feelings of isolation, disconnection, or even self-doubt. We may cling to attachments or become fearful of opening ourselves to others. Our ability to love ourselves and others diminishes, and we can feel lost between the lower and upper realms, unable to truly embrace who we are or where we're going.

But when this chakra is blocked, we may find ourselves clouded by emotions that weigh heavily on the soul: guilt, shame, jealousy, fear, anger, and insecurity. These emotions create a wall between us and the world, and between us and our true selves. We may struggle to form meaningful connections, feel distant from those we care about, or carry emotional wounds that have not yet healed. The fear of intimacy, the longing for closeness yet the hesitation to open ourselves fully. These are all signs that the heart chakra is not in harmony.

Physical symptoms may also arise from a blocked heart chakra—issues with the lungs, heart, or even respiratory system, mirroring the emotional stagnation that we may feel. When our heart is weighed down by unresolved emotions, it becomes difficult to breathe freely, to speak our truth, or to embrace the world with open arms.

Yoga poses for the heart chakra, such as the wheel pose, pigeon, and cobra, help to expand the chest and create openness in the heart space. The mantra "YAM" resonates with the heart, calling forth love, compassion, and empathy.

5. Throat Chakra (Vishuddha) – The Voice of Truth

The Gateway of Authentic Expression:

The throat chakra, or Vishuddha, is not just about the act of speaking, it's the channel through which our true voice, our inner truth, is expressed. Located at the throat, this chakra represents our ability to communicate clearly, honestly, and creatively. It is the space where our authentic self meets the world. When this chakra is balanced, we speak with confidence, express our thoughts and feelings freely, and communicate with both clarity and purpose. Our voice becomes not just a tool for interaction, but an instrument of empowerment.

The Power of Voice and Creative Expression:

Vishuddha is also the center of creativity, a place where our thoughts transform into action, and our inner world comes to life in the outer world. It is through this chakra that we give shape to our ideas, channel our passions, and express our uniqueness. It is the chakra that allows us to speak our truths, whether in words, art, or any form of creative expression. When we tap into this chakra's energy, we align with our higher selves, sharing not just information, but our essence.

The Silence of Suppression – When Vishuddha is Blocked:

However, when the throat chakra is blocked or imbalanced, it can feel like there is a disconnect between what we feel inside and what we are able to express outside. Suppressed emotions, repressed desires, and fear of judgment can prevent us from speaking up or communicating openly. This blockage can lead to feelings of frustration, a sense of being misunderstood, or even physical issues with the throat, such as a sore throat, hoarseness, or difficulty swallowing. When we are unable to express ourselves authentically, we may also experience a lack of purpose, a feeling of being disconnected from our true calling, and a general sense of creative stagnation.

The chakra's energy is deeply tied to our honesty, both with ourselves and others. When we are dishonest, either with ourselves or the world around us, it is like a weight on our throat, constricting the flow of energy and truth. To heal this chakra, we must learn to trust our voice, to speak from a place of authenticity, and to express our inner truth with courage and love.

Healing and Balancing Vishuddha:

Yoga poses like lion pose, fish pose, and shoulder stand help open the throat and allow energy to flow freely.

Sarvangasana

The mantra "HAM" reverberates through the throat, helping to awaken the energy of Vishuddha.

6. Third Eye Chakra (Ajna) – The Seat of Intuition and Inner Vision

The Gateway to Inner Wisdom:

The third eye chakra, or Ajna, located between the eyebrows, is often referred to as the seat of intuition, insight, and inner wisdom. It is a sacred space where our deeper understanding of the world and ourselves resides. This chakra is not just about intellectual knowledge, it is about the ability to see beyond the surface, to tap into the unseen realms of our consciousness, and to align with a higher truth. It is where we connect to our intuition, where clarity emerges from confusion, and where our ability to dream and manifest becomes powerful.

When the third eye chakra is open and balanced, we experience a heightened sense of awareness, a clear vision, and a deep trust in our inner guidance. We feel connected to a higher consciousness and see the world not just through our eyes, but through the lens of wisdom, understanding, and a profound sense of inner knowing. This chakra invites us to dream bigger, to see beyond our limitations, and to realize that the world is full of infinite possibilities. We start to trust in our creative power, knowing that the dreams we have within us are not just fantasies, but seeds of potential waiting to be nurtured and brought to life.

The Clouded Mind – When Ajna is Blocked:

However, when this chakra is blocked, we can feel disconnected from our intuition, as though we are wandering through life without a clear sense of direction. We may struggle with confusion, indecision, and a sense of being stuck. Our mind may become clouded, our creative vision dimmed, and we may experience headaches or even vision problems. In these moments, it's easy to feel lost, unable to see the bigger picture, and unsure of our purpose.

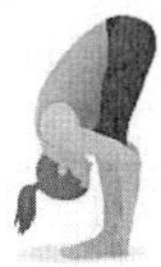

Yoga poses like Forward Fold help activate and open the Third Eye Chakra by bringing balance to the body and calming the mind. These poses create a bridge between our higher self, represented by the upper body, and our grounded, rooted self, represented by the lower body.

The Mantra of Awakening – "OM":

The chant mantra "OM" vibrates through the third eye, awakening it to its full potential. "OM" is the sound of the universe, a sacred vibration that aligns us with the divine flow of creation.

What we see with our physical eyes is merely a reflection of the surface, a fragment of a much larger reality. It's a world that we perceive through the lens of our mind and conditioned beliefs, shaped by what we've been taught, what we've experienced, and what we've allowed ourselves to believe. The illusions we encounter are not just external, but deeply intertwined with the stories we tell ourselves. We may see beauty, chaos, love, or fear, but it is all filtered through the lens of our limited perspective, our ego, and our past. And so, we often miss the truth that lies beyond, the profound connection that unites all things, the deeper meaning that transcends the material world.

Beyond Illusion – The Light of True Perception:

To awaken the third eye is to step into the light of enlightenment. It's a shift in perception, from seeing life in fragments to seeing the whole. When we connect with the third eye, we connect with a higher consciousness, an inner knowing that is not bound by time or space. It is a direct connection to truth, to love, to clarity. We no longer rely on external validation or the fleeting nature of material experiences. Instead, we trust our inner wisdom, knowing that we are always guided, always supported by the greater energy of the universe.

In that moment of awakening, the illusion fades. The world no longer appears as a series of separate, disconnected events. We see the divine intelligence that underlies everything, the interconnectedness, the flow, the infinite potential that is within us and all around us. We become free from the grip of illusion and enter into a space of limitless possibility. We are no longer prisoners of our thoughts or perceptions. We are simply present, deeply aware, and at peace with what is.

7. Crown Chakra (Sahasrara) – The Gateway to Divine Consciousness

The Thousand-Petaled Lotus of Awakening:

The crown chakra, or Sahasrara, is the gateway to the divine, the point where we transcend our physical existence and tap into the limitless consciousness that binds all things. It is the highest energy center, the connection to the cosmos, the universe, and the deepest parts of our soul. This chakra is dormant for most of us, lying untouched until we seek a deeper purpose, a more profound connection to life beyond what we see with our physical eyes.

The Seat of Universal Connection:

When the crown chakra awakens, it opens us up to an overwhelming sense of oneness with everything. It's as though we step out of the constraints of time and space, experiencing a boundless state of pure awareness. We realize that we are not separate beings, but integral parts of a greater, universal flow. This awakening brings an unexplainable joy, a joy that comes from knowing that life is not about accumulation or achievement, but about simply being. It is a profound realization of our true nature: infinite, eternal, and deeply interconnected with all that is.

Signs of Disconnection — When Sahasrara is Blocked:

But when this chakra is imbalanced, there is a deep sense of disconnection. We feel lost, spiritually confused, as though we're drifting without a compass. The world feels hollow, and no matter how much we achieve or acquire, we can never seem to find the peace or fulfillment we are searching for. This imbalance manifests physically as migraines, sleep disorders, or a lack of clarity, as we struggle to find meaning in a world that feels disconnected.

The Mantra of Cosmic Union – "AUM":

Yet, through practices like yoga, we can begin to reconnect with our higher selves. Savasana, or the Corpse Pose, is the ultimate meditation for the crown chakra. As we lie down, fully surrendering, we are reminded of the eternal truth: we came from this divine energy, and we will return to it. In this stillness, we tap into the vastness of our consciousness, shedding the burdens of the physical world, and simply being. The mantra "AUM" vibrates through us, aligning us with the frequency of the universe, grounding us in the truth that we are one with all.

The Crown of Illumination – Realizing Our True Nature:

This is the gift of the crown chakra, the understanding that we are not just individual beings, but expressions of the infinite. We are eternal, and in this realization, we find the peace we seek. There is no need for validation, for we are already connected to the highest source of wisdom, love, and truth. The crown chakra reminds us that beyond all the distractions and illusions of the world, there is only one truth: we are love, we are light, and we are eternally connected to the universe and to each other.

The Journey from Muladhara to Sahasrara:

The journey from Muladhara to Ajna, from the base of our being to the seat of our intuition and wisdom, is a profound path of awakening. Each chakra represents a step toward understanding ourselves more deeply, from our physical needs to our emotional world, and finally, to our intellect and vision. But when we reach the Ajna, the third eye chakra, we encounter a profound shift. Beyond this point, there are no established pathways, it's as though we're standing at the threshold of a new dimension, a place where the familiar laws of the physical world no longer apply. The path between Ajna and Sahasrara, the crown chakra, is a realm of pure consciousness, where we must transcend the limitations of the ego, the mind, and the body.

This is where many people find themselves stuck. They have traveled so far on the journey of self-discovery, yet when they reach the precipice of enlightenment, they falter. The challenges that once seemed conquerable become insurmountable because there is no map for this terrain. It's a space that asks for complete surrender, a letting go of everything we thought we knew, everything we thought we needed. This is the moment of true spiritual awakening, where we must trust, without reservation, in the infinite wisdom of the universe.

Peace, then, becomes not just something to attain, but the highest state of being. It's not a goal to achieve through effort or struggle, but a realization of what we already are at our core. When we truly open ourselves to the flow of life, surrendering our attachments, judgments, and desires, we discover that peace is not something we need to find outside of ourselves, it is the very essence of our being.

Peace is the bridge between the earthly and the divine, the space where the ego dissolves and the soul merges with the universe. Achieving this state requires a deep, unwavering trust in the process of life itself. We must let go of the need for control and allow ourselves to be guided by the subtle, gentle current of the divine energy that flows through us. Only then can we move beyond the limitations of the mind and step fully into the boundless, eternal peace that exists beyond the chakras, in the sacred space of Sahasrara.

And it is here, in this state of profound peace, that we find true freedom. We realize that there is nothing more to achieve, nothing more to attain, because we already are everything we need to be. Peace, in its purest form, is not a destination. It is the realization of our oneness with the universe, with all beings, and with the very essence of life itself.

The frequency of chakras:

The root chakra frequency is 396. Now keep adding +1 to the number to get higher frequencies.

396 - 417 - 528 - 639 - 741 - 852 - 963

Can a blocked chakra affect your health?

Our emotional state and the balance of our chakras are intricately connected to our physical health in ways we are only beginning to understand. Emotions such as anger, sadness, fear, jealousy, and indecisiveness are not just fleeting feelings, they are energies that ripple through our bodies, settling into our organs, our bones, our joints, and tissues. When these emotions are left unchecked, when we bottle them up or ignore them, they create blockages within the energy flow of our chakras. This blockage doesn't just stay in the energetic realm, it manifests physically, affecting the organs and systems associated with those chakras.

What begins as an emotional wound, left unhealed, can eventually show up as a physical disease. The mind and body are not separate entities; they are intertwined in ways we cannot always see, but their connection is undeniable. If we do not tend to the emotional trauma that is stored within our body, that trauma will continue to affect our health, often in ways that are beyond our conscious awareness. The body may endure for a while, but the emotional wounds we carry will eventually demand attention.

The approach we often take today is to treat the symptoms of disease, to focus on managing the physical aspect by adjusting the numbers, the lab results, and the bloodwork. Yet, this is only a temporary solution. The disease, whether it's chronic illness, pain, or fatigue, is often a reflection of deeper, unresolved emotional and energetic imbalances. And while medicine may help in bringing the body's blood chemistry back to a certain range, it doesn't address the root cause, the emotional trauma that is still festering within.

We are so often focused on fixing the surface-level disease, without recognizing that healing must go deeper. The journey of healing requires us to look inward, to confront the emotional states and unresolved trauma that we've been carrying. It requires us to release the past and open ourselves up to emotional and energetic healing. Only then can we truly restore balance to our chakras, to our energy, and to our bodies.

How can you unblock a chakra?

The journey of bringing balance to our chakras is not just about aligning the physical body; it's about aligning every part of ourselves, our thoughts, emotions, and energy. Yoga postures help us open and align our physical body, but it's the breath that becomes the true catalyst for the flow of energy through our chakras. Every conscious breath we take becomes a bridge between our inner and outer worlds, a gentle reminder that the flow of life force within us is not separate from the world around us.

Through these practices, yoga, breathwork, and meditation, we begin the sacred process of interoception, of turning our awareness inward. We start to reconnect with the sensations, the energies, and the wisdom stored within us. We remember that healing is not something we seek outside of ourselves, but something we unlock from within. As we become more attuned to our inner world, we begin to clear the blockages that hold us back, and we make space for the full expression of who we truly are.

When we raise the Kundalini, we are not just awakening a dormant energy, but an entire potential within us. It's like uncoiling the serpent of our soul, allowing our purest, most powerful energy to move freely through the chakras. As this energy rises from the root to the crown, it's as though we are reuniting with our most authentic self—awakening to our purpose, to our strength, and to our connection with the universe. We start to see the world not as something outside of us to conquer or control, but as something we are deeply connected to, something that mirrors the same energy that moves through us.

The journey to raising the Kundalini is not an easy one. It's a path that requires deep presence, patience, and trust. It's a path of transformation, of shedding the layers of fear, doubt, and emotional baggage that have accumulated over time. As we awaken this energy within, we realize that we are not simply surviving, but we are truly living. We are stepping into our full potential, embracing our true power, and aligning ourselves with the infinite source of love and light that flows through all of us.

In this space of balance and awakening, we are reminded that we are more than our thoughts, our bodies, or our circumstances. We are beings of light, of energy, and of deep interconnectedness. And as we rise, so too does the world around us. We become beacons of peace, love, and wisdom, radiating this energy outward and creating ripples of healing and transformation wherever we go.

Focus

This understanding is deeply moving because it brings us back to the heart of what it means to be truly present in our own lives. We live in a world full of distractions, constantly bombarded by information, emotions, and stimuli. At the core of it all, lies the incredible power of focus.

The Prefrontal Cortex: The Seat of Focus

Our Prefrontal Cortex, the seat of our focus, holds the key to our ability to not just exist, but to truly experience life. It's as if this part of our brain, the third eye within our forehead, is a sacred gateway to our inner world, guiding us to a deeper sense of awareness and connection. When we focus, we're not just concentrating our attention on one task; we are actively engaging in the sacred practice of being present.

Centering at the Prefrontal Cortex

When we gently bring our attention to the prefrontal cortex, the space at the center of the forehead, a subtle shift happens within. This area of the brain is responsible for focus, analysis, evaluation, and decision-making. The more we focus here, the more we become present. Grounded. Calm. Aware. Thoughts begin to slow down. Emotions begin to settle. This part of the brain is not just a structure. It is a bridge between reaction and reflection, between emotion and understanding, between chaos and clarity.

Our inner clarity starts to shine. In this still space, we become more solution-focused.

We see beyond reaction. We listen more deeply. We begin to understand the perspective of the other, not from emotion, but from awareness. This is the power of focused attention. This is the grace of coming home to the self.

Perception as the Spotlight of Attention :

What truly resonates is the idea that perception is like the spotlight of attention. What we focus on becomes our reality. If we spread our attention too thin, it becomes overwhelming. But when we choose to focus on just one thing at a time, we move into the present moment, where clarity, peace, and healing reside. In this state, we use our intellect to guide us, not as a tool of stress or anxiety, but as a source of deep insight and stillness.

The Magic of a Calm, Stable Mind:

This is where the magic of the Parasympathetic Nervous System comes into play. It is when we focus with a calm and stable mind that we begin to stimulate this system, this peaceful, healing force. The more we engage with this energy, the more we tap into the innate ability we have to heal and restore ourselves. Our bodies, minds, and spirits crave this calm. It is the space where true healing occurs, where our systems reset and we come back into harmony with ourselves.

The realization is deep that focusing our attention in a positive, singular way can stimulate the parasympathetic nervous system. It reminds us that peace isn't something to be searched for externally, but something to be nurtured and cultivated within. It calls us to slow down, to breathe deeply, and to choose where we place our focus, knowing that this act alone holds the power to heal, to calm, and to guide us toward a deeper state of well-being.

Cultivating a Parasympathetic Mind:

So, let us embrace this wisdom and allow ourselves to focus on the present moment. Let us create space for stillness and awareness. And as we do, we will not only find the peace we are seeking but will also discover the incredible power within us to heal, transform, and live fully.

The more we focus, the more we are in the present moment, the more we are using our intellect, the more is the Parasympathetic stimulated, the more we are relaxed, the more we heal.

A concentrated mind is a focused mind and only a stable calm mind can achieve this.

This means Parasympathetic stimulation will achieve a calm mind. Hence a PARASYMPATHETIC MIND

Let's focus on how to stimulate my Parasympathetic Nervous system.

Remember the golden rule of the parasympathetic system: it increases secretions. Now let's apply it to each organ one by one

1. **Breathing -**

Cyclic ventilation:

Inhalations = Exhalations

Cyclic ventilation, in its simplest form, is a process where ventilation (air exchange) alternates in cycles, often used in various settings such as mechanical ventilation for patients. But when we think about it emotionally, it almost feels like a rhythmic dance between life and breath.

The idea of cycles, of inhaling and exhaling reminds us of how we, as humans, move through phases in life. There are times when we take in new experiences, new lessons, new breaths. And there are moments when we need to exhale, to release the weight of what we've taken in, to let go. It's a balance between receiving and giving, taking care of ourselves, and nourishing the world around us.

Cyclic ventilation represents that delicate balance, where each breath is purposeful and necessary, each cycle sustaining life, ensuring we don't run out of air, or run out of hope. It's like the ebb and flow of emotions, where we sometimes feel overwhelmed, and other times, we find release, only to go through it all again.

It's not just about air, it's about the cycles we live through.

Sympathetic Breathing:

Inhalations > Exhalations

In yogic tradition (particularly *swara yoga*), it's said that:

Right nostril dominance (Pingala nadi) is linked with solar, heating, active energy, often compared with the **sympathetic nervous system** (alertness, action, outward focus).

Left nostril dominance (Ida nadi) is linked with lunar, cooling, calming energy, compared with the **parasympathetic nervous system** (rest, relaxation, inward focus).

Modern science also supports aspects of this:

Studies show that **unilateral nostril breathing** can influence autonomic activity.

Right nostril breathing tends to **increase heart rate, blood pressure, and oxygen consumption,** suggesting sympathetic activation.

Left nostril breathing tends to **decrease heart rate and enhance relaxation,** indicating parasympathetic activation.

Right nostril → sympathetic activation.

Left nostril → parasympathetic activation.

The Transformative Power of Breath:

It's so profound to realize that something as simple as our breath has the power to trigger a cascade of changes within us, shaping how we feel, think, and respond to the world around us.

The connection between deep inhales and adrenaline release is such a beautiful reminder of the body's wisdom. When we take in a long, deep breath, it's as though we are filling ourselves with energy, alertness, and a readiness to face whatever lies ahead. It's as though our breath is preparing us for action, priming us to meet the moment with all of our senses heightened and our minds sharp.

But what's even more touching is the idea that the way we breathe can also tell us where we are emotionally and mentally. If our inhales are longer, more aggressive, and more intense than our exhales, we become more alert, more activated and at times, more anxious or overwhelmed. Our bodies are essentially signaling to us, letting us know that we may be in a heightened state of arousal or stress.

Reading the Body through Breath:

It's in this awareness that the real power lies. By simply becoming conscious of our breath, we can tap into our inner state and influence it. If we notice that we're holding tension, or if we feel overly stimulated, we can gently shift our breathing, creating a longer, slower exhale to invite calmness, release, and balance. It's as if we can take control of the energy flowing through us, steering it toward a place of peace.

This subtle yet profound connection between breath and body speaks volumes about our ability to shape our experience. It's an invitation to tune into the rhythm of our breath, to notice how it flows and responds to the world around us, and to use it as a tool to guide ourselves back to balance whenever we feel out of sync. In this way, breath becomes more than just a biological function; it becomes a bridge between our physical and emotional worlds, a beautiful and natural way to find peace in the midst of chaos.

Meditative Parasympathetic Breathing :

Inhalations < Exhalations

The meditative practice involves slow breathing: controlled inhale, breath-hold, long exhale, breath-hold.

The Rhythm of Inner Awareness:

In normal circumstances, our breath flows easily, with active inhalation and passive exhalation. It's natural and effortless, like the rhythm of life itself. But when we engage in meditative breathing, we enter into a space where we take control, where the rhythm changes and becomes intentional, deliberate, and deeply healing. The passive, short inhalation followed by the active, long exhalation is a key that unlocks the door to profound inner awareness.

As we focus on this breathing pattern, we shift our awareness inward, guiding ourselves into a state of deep interoception. The movement of the diaphragm becomes the focal point, as we feel it rise and fall, pushing us into that sacred space of stillness. In this act of conscious exhalation, we are not just letting go of air; we are letting go of stress, tension, and all the weight we carry in our bodies and minds. It's like a wave of calm washing over us, creating space for clarity, peace, and healing.

And in this moment, as we continue to focus on our breath, we stimulate the parasympathetic nervous system awakening the body's natural ability to relax, to restore, and to find balance. The more we practice, the more we strengthen our connection to this soothing force, embracing the power of our breath to bring us back to the present moment, to the space of calm, to a place where we can truly heal.

This is the beauty of mindfulness in action, how something as simple as our breath can be transformed into a source of immense power and healing. In this sacred space of breath, we can let go, surrender, and return to ourselves. And in doing so, we invite peace into every cell of our being.

2. Yoga as a Path to Inner Stillness :

When we quiet the body, we also create stillness in the mind. Yoga becomes a practice of harmonizing the inner and outer worlds, where physical postures serve not just to stretch or strengthen, but to bring us to a place of peace and presence.

It's as if, through these poses, we are not just training our bodies, but we are learning to "be" in the moment, to let go of all distractions, and to allow ourselves simply to exist in a state of peaceful awareness.

The Paradox of Active Calm

To think that we can engage in a physical practice that generates sweat, raises our heart rate, and yet still cultivates calm is nothing short of miraculous. It's a beautiful reminder that movement doesn't always need to be frantic or rushed to be powerful. By integrating breath, mindfulness, and intention, we can move and sweat without the chaos of our sympathetic nervous system taking over. Instead, we can invoke a calm energy, a grounding presence that centers us, no matter the pace of the movement.

Yoga invites us to return to ourselves, to connect deeply with our own essence. It teaches us that true strength lies not in force or speed, but in the ability to remain grounded, still, and open, even in the midst of movement.

Activating Core and Energy Centers :

This practice is so beautifully transformative. Yoga, at its deepest level, is about tuning into the internal rhythm of the body, reconnecting with the energy centers that drive our emotions, actions, and sense of self: the core muscles, which hold not just our physical structure but also our emotional and energetic states, are activated in each pose, working to open and balance our chakras. The heart chakra, where love and compassion flow; the solar plexus chakra, the seat of personal power; the sacral chakra, where creativity and pleasure reside; and the root chakra, which grounds us to the earth.

As we engage these centers, we begin to feel more whole, more aligned with our true selves. There is an almost magical quality to how the body starts to respond when we consciously connect with each chakra through movement and breath. The interoceptive focus allows us to deeply listen to the inner sensations, to feel the subtle shifts within the body, and to observe how the mind follows suit, becoming quieter and clearer with each inhale and exhale.

Box Breathing and Flow:

When we combine this mindful movement with box breathing, holding the breath and releasing it slowly, intentionally, we are not just increasing our physical endurance but also cultivating inner calm. The sweat that pours from our bodies is not just a sign of exertion; it's a release of tension, a letting go of stored emotions and energy. As our heart rate rises, the body becomes alive with energy, and yet through focused breath, we create a balance, a flow of energy that nurtures rather than depletes.

This combination of movement, breath, and intention is a beautiful reminder of our interconnectedness. The way our physical, emotional, and spiritual selves are woven together. When we practice yoga with full presence, we not only strengthen our body but also heal, open, and expand our inner landscape, ultimately becoming more attuned to who we truly are.

3. Meditation – the art of returning to self:

Meditation is truly the art of returning to ourselves. It is a journey into stillness, a space where the chatter of the world falls away and we are left with nothing but the pure essence of our being. The word "Dhyana" from Sanskrit, "Meditat" from Latin, they all point to the same truth: the power of contemplation. But contemplation isn't just about thinking or pondering, it's about feeling, being, and simply existing in the present moment.

The Journey Inward: Stillness and Focus:

In order to contemplate deeply, we need focus. But that focus can only arise from a place of inner calm, a stillness that allows us to look inward without distraction. Imagine the mind as a turbulent ocean. When it's choppy, it's hard to see anything clearly beneath the surface. But when the water stills, the clarity becomes undeniable. Meditation is like finding that calm within ourselves. It's a quieting of the storms, a softening of the constant noise and clutter that fills our mind.

When we reach this stillness, it's as if time slows down. Our thoughts become less about the past and future, and more about the simple truth of now. In that state, we tap into something far deeper—our true self, free from the weight of external demands and expectations. It's a return to peace, to clarity, to an almost sacred space where we can simply be. And in that space, we realize that our answers lie not in thinking, but in just being.

Swarajya Meditation: Ruling over the Self

Swarajya Meditation is a beautiful and empowering practice that teaches us the art of self-mastery. Swarajya, a term that literally translates to "ruling over Self", is the foundation of true inner freedom. In a world full of distractions, it's so easy to lose sight of our inner peace, but through this meditation, we remember that the power to find calm and clarity has always been within us.

Padmasana: The Posture of Presence

When we sit in Padmasana, or Lotus Pose, we are not just sitting; we are making a conscious choice to be present. By gently placing each foot on the opposite thigh and sitting with a straight, strong spine, we create a physical foundation of stability. This posture symbolizes our connection to the earth, while the upright spine reflects our connection to the higher realms. In this posture, we are rooted, yet elevated.

Breath as a Gateway to Stillness:

As we focus on our breath, the practice becomes a gentle yet powerful reminder that in order to still the mind, we must first still the body. The slow, deliberate inhalations and exhalations guide us into a space where time slows down. The abdominal breathing, filling the abdomen with air as we inhale, and drawing it inward as we exhale, helps center us, grounding us in the present moment.

When we practice this, there's a quieting of the body and, slowly, the mind follows. With each breath, the noise of the world falls away, leaving us with only the stillness of our inner being. This is the beauty of Swarajya Meditation, through focusing on the breath, we gradually bring our scattered thoughts into alignment, allowing us to achieve the peace and stillness that lies at the core of who we are.

When we meditate there are three stages to it.

Stage One: Establishing a Relationship with the Self:

The journey of meditation is a deeply transformative one, and it all begins with the first step: **Establishing a relationship with the SELF.** It asks us the most important question we can ever ask ourselves: **Who am I?**

For most of us, our instinctive response is, "I am my body," because that's the world we see, touch, and experience. But when we take a step back and reflect, we realize that the body is just a vessel, an instrument. There's something much deeper within. That "I", that awareness, that presence, that energy, is the real essence of who we are. This energy is what animates the body, what gives life to the mind, what governs the intellect, and what fuels our emotions. I am not my body; I am the energy that runs through it.

In meditation, we begin by nurturing this connection to the SELF. We understand that we are not just flesh and bones; we are light, pure, and radiant. When we turn inward, we start to recognize ourselves as beings of light, a shining star in the center of our forehead. This light is the source of our strength, peace, and power. It radiates calmness and happiness. We are not just passive beings caught in the ebb and flow of life. We are the rulers of our own being.

Through this meditation, we affirm: **I am a powerful being, I am a happy being, I am a peaceful being.** These words are not just mantras, but truths that reflect the essence of who we are. The mind, intellect, and sanskars, these are all parts of us, but they do not define us. We are the silent observer of all these aspects, the one who holds the reins and directs the course of our life.

When we deeply understand this truth, that we are the energy, the pure light, everything changes. We begin to see beyond the surface. We stop identifying ourselves with temporary emotions or physical states. We start to understand that true peace and happiness come from within, from recognizing and connecting to the radiant light that we truly are.

In this space, meditation becomes not just a practice, but a way of life, a way of being. As we sit in stillness, we remember this light within and begin to embody it. Every thought, every feeling, every breath becomes a reflection of this truth: *I am light, I am energy, I am the ruler of my own being.* And with this realization, we experience a deep sense of empowerment, peace, and purpose.

Stage Two: Connecting with the Supreme Father:

It is a sacred and transformative process. If I am energy, if I am light, it makes perfect sense that I need to connect with the ultimate energy, the source of all light. A stone idol cannot embody the energy I seek, because I am not stone; I am the living, vibrant, radiant energy that flows within me. And the Supreme Father, too, is not just a distant figure, but the brightest and most powerful point of light, a light that is beyond our comprehension, glowing with the warmth of golden-red radiance.

In this deep connection, I, the humble point of light, reach out to the Supreme Father, who is the eternal source of all that is pure, wise, and loving. As I stand in my light, I recognize that I am drawn to His brilliance, His divine radiance, to be replenished, nourished, and empowered. The light that I receive from Him does not just illuminate my path, it fills me with grace, with peace, with strength.

In my communication with the Supreme Father, I bow in gratitude. **I thank You, Lord,** for each new day that brings the gift of life, for every breath I take that nourishes my being, for every step I walk in the light of Your wisdom. I am grateful for the knowledge You provide, for the guidance You offer, and for the lessons You allow me to learn. Each moment, each encounter, is a reflection of Your love and care.

With every meal, with every drink, I am reminded of Your constant provision. **You, my Supreme Father, are the giver of everything, the sustainer of all that is.** And in this awareness, I feel deeply connected to You. **I, the point of light, am eternally connected to You, the supreme point of light.**

This relationship with the Supreme Father fills me with love, gratitude, and a deep sense of belonging. It's not about worship in the conventional sense; it's about an inner, soul-deep connection where I recognize that I am never alone. I am supported, guided, and embraced by a love that is beyond measure. The light I receive from You fills me, strengthens me, and radiates outward, connecting me with all beings and with the world around me.

And with this light, I am reminded of my true purpose,to shine, to love, to serve, and to reflect the divine radiance I have so graciously received.

Stage Three: Harmonizing Relationships with Others:

Our connections with others are reflections of the energy we put out into the world. When we understand that we receive what we give, it becomes clear that the energy I send out, whether consciously or unconsciously, will return to me in different forms.

If I am receiving anger from someone, it is not just a random occurrence. It is a mirror reflecting the anger I may have unknowingly sent out. The power to change begins with me. I must take responsibility for my own actions and energy. The first step is to acknowledge this truth, **if I have received negativity, I must have, at some point, contributed to it.**

In this moment of realization, **I choose to ask for forgiveness**. I ask for forgiveness from those I have hurt, knowingly or unknowingly, through my words, my actions, or my energy. By doing so, I open my heart to healing and transformation. I recognize that healing begins when I take ownership of my own energy and commit to doing better.

When anger arises in me, I pause and reflect. I understand that this emotion may be rooted in something I've previously sent out into the world. I remind myself that everything happening to me is perfect, it is a consequence of what I have given, and now I have the opportunity to choose differently.

Now, with this awareness, I shift my focus. I make the choice to give kindness, patience, and understanding. If I want people to treat me with respect, I will treat them with the same respect. If I wish to receive love, I will give love. If I want peace, I will give peace.

I begin to live with the awareness that everything I do, every thought I have, and every emotion I feel is a seed I am planting. And I must be mindful of the seeds I plant, for they will grow and return to me in the form of my relationships with others. As I consciously choose to send out positive energy, I invite more positivity into my life.

In this way, I take responsibility not only for my actions but for the energy I share with the world. And through this process of giving and receiving, I cultivate deeper, more harmonious connections with everyone around me, fostering an environment of love, understanding, and mutual respect. **I am the change I wish to see in my relationships, and through my actions, I create the love and peace I seek.**

In the first two stages, I begin by visualizing myself as a point of pure white light, and the Supreme Father as a brilliant, golden-red light. At first, I consciously create this thought, feeling the connection between my light and the Supreme's light. Each time I practice this, I can feel the bond growing stronger, deeper, and more profound. As I continue to do this, something beautiful begins to happen. I no longer need to create the thought. The connection becomes natural, effortless, and intuitive.

It is as though my being has attuned itself to the frequency of divine energy, and I no longer need to remind myself of it. This silent connection blooms within me, and I feel it in every part of my being, guiding me toward a state of inner peace. This is the beginning of something profound. **I am no longer separated from the divine. I am united with it.**

As I progress further, I reach the next stage—the stage where I am not creating any thoughts. There is only silence. Absolute stillness. In this space, I am beyond thoughts, beyond words. The world outside may continue with its noise, its chaos, but inside, I am perfectly still. **I am in a state of pure bliss.** The silence is not empty; it is filled with divine presence, filled with an overwhelming sense of peace. **This is where true freedom lies, freedom from the noise of the world, freedom from the incessant chatter of the mind.**

And then, there comes the final stage, the stage of complete alignment with the Supreme Father. I can now remain in this state of stillness even amidst the noise of the world. External circumstances no longer disturb me. I am not swayed by what happens around me. Nothing affects me. My inner world remains untouched by the chaos of the outer world. In this moment, I am deeply aligned with the Supreme Lord, and His presence fills every part of my being. I am not merely a person seeking peace; I have become peace itself.

This is the beauty of spiritual practice. As I move through these stages, I come to realize that true alignment with the divine does not require external conditions to be perfect. **It only requires a deep commitment to stilling the mind, silencing the heart, and connecting with the divine light within.** And in that silence, in that connection, I find **bliss,** and in that bliss, I find everything I've ever longed for.

Meditation *is not a technique.* It is a **surrender.** It neither binds the soul nor ties it down, but fills every moment with **divinity.** When we leave our thoughts behind, **God does not appear in waiting...** but in **silence.** To meditate is to live in the **now,** no fear of the future, no burden of the past. Just one quiet curiosity remains: **Who am I? Meditation** is a state where **the soul gazes upon the soul.** There is no speech. No thought. Only **presence.** It is as if **silence begins to breathe.**

Meditation as Tapasya – The Sacred Fire Within

In the ancient language of the soul, meditation is not just silence. It is not escape, nor stillness for its own sake. It is known as Yog Bhatti or Tapasya, a sacred inner fire. Just as raw gold is placed into flames to purify and shine, so too, the soul enters meditation to burn away what no longer serves.

Anger, fear, pain, and past identities are all gently offered into this inner fire. Meditation is not always soft. Sometimes, it is fierce. Because to be reborn, something must be shed. To become light, we must release the weight we carry. This Bhatti, this Tapasya, is not outer ritual, but inner transformation. A pyre, where the old self dissolves, and a new awareness arises. In this sacred heat, the ego melts, resistance fades, and the soul begins to shine not with borrowed light, but with its own radiance. To meditate is to sit in this sacred fire, not to be consumed, but to be purified. Not to be destroyed, but to be revealed. Meditation is the flame in the temple no one sees, yet it lights the entire being from within. It doesn't chase away darkness; it transforms it, revealing that even shadows belong to the light. At the threshold of your existence, God waits… not with answers, but with presence. For the soul does not speak in words; it speaks in stillness, in patience, in the quiet knowing that what you seek has always been seeking you. The mind screams: "Look! Search! Shout! Prove!" But the soul whispers: "Be still. Let go. Fall in." And so the question shifts, not "Can you find God?" but "Can you bear to live without Him?" The Divine is not found in the running but in the resting. The more you chase Him outside, the more the path stretches endlessly. But when you stop, when you listen, He is there in the breath, between the heartbeats, in the silence you tried to fill. When all outer roads lead only to more questions… you are returned, empty, to the temple within. And it is there, when even thought has collapsed, and you can do nothing but be, that meditation happens not as effort, but as grace. When inner darkness deepens to the point of blindness, it is then that the unseen hand lights the lamps of stillness. Not because you found God, but because you finally stopped hiding. The self, as you knew it, begins to dissolve. Boundaries blur. Stories fade. And in that melting, a silence rises not empty, but alive. Peace arrives, not as stillness, but as a sacred storm that strips away all that is false. And when everything flows away, what remains is not a name, not a thought, not even you, but the eternal. In meditation, what is lost is only illusion, and what is found was never truly gone. You vanish as form, but awaken as presence. When ego, desire, identity dissolve, what remains is not emptiness, but truth stripped of all masks. There is no language here, no doctrine, only the fire of silence where the known dies and the eternal awakens. The third eye does not see outward, but it witnesses within. When the outer gaze collapses from exhaustion and longing, a new vision is born clear, vast, and wordless. And then, the final truth begins to whisper: You are not what you see.

The third eye does not open by force; it opens when everything else falls away. A thought comes; you see it, you smile, you let it go. No resistance. No judgment. Just the grace of allowing. This is the current of meditation, not a river you swim, but one that carries you. The more you surrender, the more the river knows the way. You don't need to reach the shore; the shore comes to you. Witnessing is the invisible ladder that rises not from the ground but from stillness and it doesn't take you away from life; it lifts you into the sky within it. The sky of pure awareness, open, endless, free. When meditation becomes silence, and silence deepens beyond sound, time stops. The illusion of sequence falls away. There is no day or night, no past, no future, not even now. There is only that which contains it all, yet is untouched by all. Memory clings, but silence lets go. Silence holds no story, no past, and no name. In the true zero, you do not exist as you once thought yourself to be. This is the silence that questions not with words, but with its very presence, a silence so deep, even the desire to survive fades. Until now, you were walking the path; now, you have become the path itself. Until now, you were listening for silence; now, you are the silence from which all sounds arise and fall. Meditation is no longer something you do, it is what you are. The seeker has vanished. The journey has dissolved. Only this remains pure, unmoving, luminous. You are no longer the flame reaching for the sky; you are the sky that holds the flame, the space where nothing is missing and nothing is held. Now, there is nothing to become. There is only to be, and in that being, existence itself begins to bloom through you. This is not the end. This is the still beginning of everything.

4. Tratak:

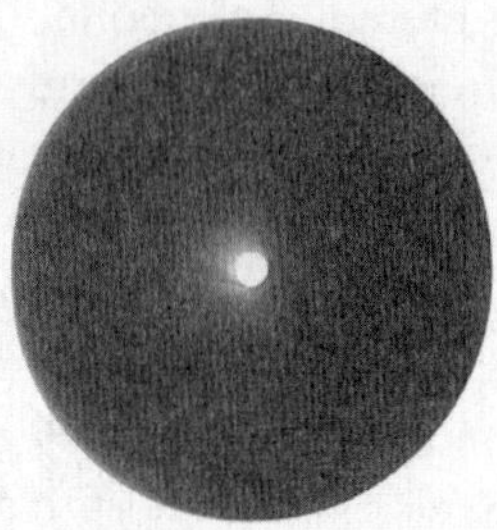

Tratak, the sacred practice of gaze, is not just a simple act of staring at an object; it is a journey of deepening our awareness and nurturing our inner power. When we engage in Tratak, we focus our attention on a single point, a flame, a symbol, or any object of choice, and in doing so, we begin to quiet the noise of the world around us. It's like a moment of pure connection between our body, mind, and spirit.

Fixing the Gaze: Diving Within :

As we fix our gaze, we are not just looking at an object; we are diving deep within ourselves. Tratak cultivates concentration, our mind becomes sharper, more focused. We feel the rush of clarity, allowing us to be more productive in everything we do. Every task, no matter how big or small, becomes an opportunity to channel our energy with intention.

And with that focus, we find a beautiful side effect: stress begins to melt away. Our mind finds a sense of peace that has long been missing. The worries, the anxiety, the endless rush of thoughts, they all fade into the background as we become absorbed in this simple act of being present with the flame, the point, the object. The tension that once seemed so overwhelming gives way to calm, and in that space, we reconnect with a deeper sense of serenity.

Benefits:

The benefits of Tratak go even further. With consistent practice, memory and cognitive abilities strengthen, as if the act of focusing sharpens not just our vision but our whole mind. We feel more intuitive, more connected to our inner wisdom. Decisions that once felt clouded and uncertain become clear, and with clarity comes the power to move forward with confidence.

This simple practice, with its focus on an object, even helps improve our vision. The strengthening of the eye muscles and the optic nerve is a reminder of the mind-body connection: our inner clarity has the ability to affect our external world. As we engage in Tratak, we start seeing more than just the object before us; we begin to see with a clearer vision, not just physically but mentally, emotionally, and spiritually.

Morning Practice: Setting the Tone for the Day:

By practicing Tratak in the early morning, we start the day with a sense of peace, setting the tone for everything that follows. And in those moments, even if our gaze falters or our eyes blink, it doesn't matter. What matters is that we return. We always return to the focus, the calm, the clarity. In this sacred return, we are training ourselves to stay present, to let go of distractions, and to reclaim the stillness that resides within us.

The Power of Returning: Training the Mind

The beauty of this practice lies in its simplicity: the more we wander and the more we gently bring our focus back, the more we are training our minds. Every time our attention drifts, we are not failing; we are learning. We are strengthening our ability to return, to center ourselves again in the present moment. This process of refocusing, again and again, is like an inner workout, allowing our mind to grow stronger and more resilient. It's a quiet and powerful form of self-mastery, this is neuroplasticity at work.

In the beginning, the refocusing might feel like a challenge, like a constant pull of the mind to wander, but with practice, it becomes almost effortless. Over time, the mind becomes more attuned to the act of focus, and the distractions we once gave so much energy to no longer hold the same power. Eventually, our attention shifts naturally without resistance, as if we've trained our brain to know that focus is our true state.

The Body's Response: Tears, Energy, and Healing:

As we deepen our practice and extend the duration of our gaze, the physical body begins to react in ways that show us how interconnected our systems are. The eyes, once tired, now begin to water, and the energy flows from within us in the form of tears. It's as though our body is releasing, releasing stress, releasing tension, and allowing the energy to move. And even when tears roll down our cheeks, it's not simply a sympathetic reaction. There's something more profound happening here. This is a parasympathetic response, a sign that the body is entering a state of deep relaxation and healing. The release is gentle, subtle, and soothing.

Each tear, each gentle moment of focus, reminds us that in this practice, we are not just training the mind. We are reprogramming ourselves, rewiring our responses, and connecting deeply to the stillness within. This practice doesn't just change us mentally, but physically and emotionally too. It is the art of becoming whole, of refining and rebalancing every part of ourselves.

5. Mindful Eating: Honoring the Body and Energy:

The Hidden Power of Eating:

There's something deeply profound about the simple act of eating, something that often goes unnoticed in our daily routines. Most of us have gotten into the habit of watching TV, scrolling through our phones, or distracting ourselves with thoughts while we eat. But when we do this, we're not just multitasking; we're unknowingly triggering our sympathetic nervous system, activating stress, and disconnecting from the present moment. Our bodies, in this state of distraction, don't receive the nourishment they truly need.

Eating with a mind engaged elsewhere dampens our body's natural responses. Salivation slows, and our stomach doesn't receive the full benefit of the digestive enzymes that help break down our food. The richness of the process is lost. But when we eat mindfully, when we focus on each bite, savoring the texture, the flavor, the warmth, we awaken our parasympathetic nervous system, the one that encourages relaxation and healing.

Savoring Each Bite:

There's beauty in this awareness, in paying attention to the small but significant act of chewing. When we take the time to chew slowly, to feel the food in our mouth, to notice the subtle way saliva increases and blends with the food, we begin to notice that the process of digestion starts right there, in our mouths. The salivation, which might have been neglected during distracted eating, begins to flow naturally. And with each bite, we become more connected, more present to the nourishment our food offers.

I know it can feel challenging at first, 32 chews may seem like a lot. It's easy to get discouraged or feel like it's too much work. But when we allow ourselves the space to truly experience the food, to focus solely on that moment, we create a deeper sense of satisfaction, not just in our bodies, but in our souls.

The act of chewing slowly is a practice of mindfulness, one that teaches us how to truly be in the moment, appreciating each morsel, and allowing our bodies to fully benefit from what we consume. Eating mindfully is a small but powerful reminder that we are deserving of the time and attention it takes to care for ourselves, truly and wholly.

Energy Flow Through the Throat Chakra:

When I eat, I can visualize my throat chakra awakening. The act of chewing and swallowing ignites energy in this space, fueling the digestive process. This is an energy that should be directed solely towards digestion, towards nourishing my body. But then, if my focus shifts, as if I'm distracted by a television show or the news, my sympathetic nervous system starts to activate, drawing my attention away from the digestive process. Suddenly, energy that was meant for my body's nourishment is now being pulled in different directions, causing a kind of dissonance in my energy flow.

This is a powerful reminder of how important it is to be mindful of what I'm focusing on when I'm eating. If I allow my attention to drift, I'm not only missing the opportunity to nourish my body properly but also distributing my energy unevenly, which can disrupt my overall balance.

Aligning with Daily Rhythms:

And then, there's the way we handle our energy throughout the day versus the night. During the day, our bodies are energized, active, and our core temperature rises with activity. But when the day winds down, it's essential to create a shift in our energy to allow for rest. This is why it's recommended that we allow a two-hour gap between our evening meal and bedtime. If I eat too close to bedtime, the energy needed for digestion is directed towards the solar chakra, activating the digestive process at a time when it should be winding down. By giving myself this gap, I am allowing my body to prepare for rest, to reduce the heat within, and to enter into a state that supports deep, restorative sleep.

We are so connected to our body's rhythms, and when we listen, when we respect these natural flows, we allow ourselves to fully thrive. It's in these small, mindful moments, whether it's being present with our meal or allowing time for digestion before sleep, that we honor our body's deepest needs. I'm learning to be more mindful of where I place my energy, knowing that the more I align with these rhythms, the more balanced, peaceful, and whole I feel.

6. Vagal Nerve Stimulation:

The Vagus nerve is truly a silent yet powerful force within us, acting as a bridge between our mind and body. When I think about how it originates at the base of the brain and travels all the way down to the abdomen, it's like a pathway, carrying life-sustaining messages from within.

Healing Through Sound:

One of the most profound ways to connect with the Vagus nerve is through sound. Singing, humming, or even chanting "OM"—such simple acts, yet they create such a deep sense of relaxation. The vibration of the sound reaches inside, slows heart rate, and eases the tension in the body. When we are overwhelmed, a simple hum can bring us back to ourselves. It's as if we are reminding our bodies to relax, to soften, to let go. We can feel our breath gently shifting, our pulse slowing, and a calmness washing over us.

Cold Exposure and Vagus Activation:

Then there's the concept of cold exposure. When we immerse ourselves in cold, whether it's a cold shower or an ice bath, the Vagus nerve is awakened in a way that we never expected. It's like a jolt of life, of clarity. Yes, it's intense, but in that intensity, there's a stillness that follows, a moment of profound peace. The cold helps quiet the noise inside, slow the rush of thoughts, and bring us back to a deeper connection within.

These practices help us to reconnect with ourselves. They teach us that the path to relaxation, to peace, and to being truly present is not about escaping the world around us, but instead, about gently bringing our attention inward, where true calm resides. The Vagus nerve, this hidden connection within, is a reminder that we have the power to soothe ourselves, to heal, and to find peace in the simplest of actions.

Breathing as a Pathway to Calm:

When I think about deep breathing, it feels almost like reconnecting with my soul. Holding the breath, whether for 20 seconds or a full minute, creates a space of pause that's so healing. In the stillness of that moment, I am reminded that everything will be okay. Abdominal breathing, with its gentle rise and fall of the belly, helps me soften and release all the tightness I carry in my body. It's as if I'm breathing life back into myself, clearing away the fog of stress and anxiety. I feel calmer, centered, and more present with each inhale and exhale.

Self-Massage and Touch:

Massaging the Vagus nerve, gently pressing in front and behind the ears, feels almost like self-compassion. It's a physical act, yet it feels deeply nurturing. We can feel the tension slip away as our bodies sigh in relief as if to say, "I've got you." This simple touch becomes a way of honoring our needs, reminding ourselves that it's okay to slow down and care for ourselves.

Gargling and Vocal Vibrations:

And then there's the power of sound. Gargling with water or even singing out loud. At first, it feels playful, almost silly but then we realize, it's deeply grounding. The vibration of our voice and sound resonance activates the vagus nerve, sending waves of calm and peace throughout the body.

When we think about connecting with others, there's something deeply profound about the way relationships nourish our souls. Genuine, heart-centered connections have a way of filling the space with warmth, understanding, and joy. It's in the shared moments, the laughter, and even the vulnerability, that we find ourselves truly seen and heard. As we nurture these relationships, we feel this surge of happiness, not just because of the bond, but because we are reminded of the beauty of shared humanity. In those moments, the vagus nerve is activated, creating a deep sense of calm and peace within our bodies. It's as if love itself is the current that runs through us, soothing all the tensionand allowing us to breathe more freely.

Focusing our minds and being present with those we care about, helps us escape the constant swirl of negative thoughts that can cloud our minds. The past, with its regrets, or the future, with its worries, no longer dominates our thoughts. Instead, we are here, fully engaged, and our energy is not scattered but collected. It feels like we are conserving precious life force, allowing our thoughts to be intentional, purposeful, and positive.

In these moments, it feels like we are truly living, not just existing, but thriving in the energy of love, connection, and focused intention. The power of connecting with others, of engaging in meaningful relationships, is not just about boosting happiness, it's about giving ourselves the space to feel, to grow, and to truly be alive.

CHAPTER 7

MYSTERIOUS MIND

Autopilot Living:

It's incredible to realize that the way we have been reacting to situations, the way we have been navigating through life, is not always as conscious as we thought. For so long, we have been comfortable in this routine, where our responses have become automated. It almost feels as if we have been operating on autopilot, simply reacting to life as it comes, without truly questioning if this is the best way to live. But when we step back and reflect, we realize that many of our reactions, these automatic responses, have been influenced by thoughts that are not always pure, not always positive. And over time, these thoughts have started to affect not just our internal state, but the way we interact with the world and the people we care about.

Radiating Energy:

The truth is that every thought we create comes with an emotion attached to it. That emotion doesn't just stay with us; it radiates outward. It affects the person for whom it was created, whether it's love, kindness, or, unfortunately, frustration and anger. These emotions, in turn, influence our relationships, often without us even being fully aware of it. We become caught in a loop of creating the same emotions, and those emotions shape our perspective on everything around us. We start seeing the world through that emotional filter, and that filter colors how we experience each moment.

It's also striking how much those emotions begin to affect our physical health. The stress, the negativity, the unresolved feelings, they eventually manifest in our body. We may not realize it, but our heart, our stomach, even our immune system are bearing the weight of emotions we haven't fully processed or healed. This emotional energy radiates not only in our body and relationships but out into the world around us, shaping the energy of our home, the atmosphere of our environment, and the world at large.

The Journey of Emotional Healing:

It's clear now that we have the power to shift how we respond. We don't need to remain trapped in automated reactions. We can choose to shift our thoughts, to choose purity, kindness, and compassion in the way we think and react. When we do that, not only do we feel lighter, but our relationships feel more harmonious, our physical health improves, and the energy we radiate can help shift the world around us, creating a more positive and peaceful atmosphere.

Change is not easy, but it's necessary for growth. By bringing awareness to our thoughts and emotions, we can begin to heal, to let go of old patterns, and to create a new reality where we respond with love, understanding, and clarity. This journey of self-awareness and emotional healing is not just for us, it's for everyone we touch, for every relationship we engage in, and for the energy we contribute to the universe.

This is the famous depiction of a chariot with the horses and the charioteer.

The Chariot Metaphor:

The image of the chariot is so deeply powerful, isn't it? It beautifully illustrates the intricate relationship between the senses, the mind, and the intellect. When I reflect on it, I realize how much this chariot metaphor resonates with my own life.

The horses, representing my senses, are wild and untamed, constantly pulling me in different directions with what I see, hear, taste, touch, and smell. They can be overwhelming, leading me to react impulsively or get distracted by fleeting desires. Without a steady hand guiding them, my senses can easily run wild, pulling me away from what truly matters.

The Reins of the Mind:

Then there's the mind, the reins that try to control the horses. But if my mind is distracted, restless, or out of control, the horses will run off in whatever direction they please. The reins lose their strength, and I lose my focus. The mind, in its natural state, can often be chaotic and unruly.

The Charioteer: Intellect in Action:

But the true strength comes from the charioteer, the intellect. The intellect is my inner wisdom, the stillness and clarity that has the power to guide the reins and keep my senses in check. If my intellect is strong and clear, it can steer the horses of my senses, keeping them focused on what truly matters. It's not about suppressing my senses, but rather, allowing the intellect to guide me in using them consciously and purposefully.

Empowerment Through Choice:

When my intellect is in control, I am not at the mercy of my impulses or distractions. I can rule over my mind and emotions instead of being ruled by them. I can make decisions with clarity, purpose, and calm. It's in those moments that I truly feel empowered, not by what I see or what I feel in the moment, but by my ability to choose my responses, to rise above the chaos, and to guide myself towards what aligns with my highest good.

This chariot analogy reminds me that no matter how wild my senses or my mind might feel at times, I have the power within me to reclaim control. With a steady hand and a clear mind, I can steer my life in the direction I desire.

The Brain's Vault:

The quality of the information I take in shapes my thoughts and emotional responses. It's as if every moment I'm absorbing, storing, and internalizing so much, whether consciously or unconsciously, that it becomes the foundation for how I experience life. The hippocampus, this remarkable part of my brain, is like a vault, holding on to every bit of information I've ever encountered. It has this incredible role in preserving the essence of my experiences, my lessons, and my memories.

When I think about it, every emotion, every reaction I've had in the past, has been influenced by what's been stored in that vault. The memories I've stored, the way I've processed them, and the quality of the information I've absorbed all play a part in shaping how I respond to new situations. It's no wonder that when faced with a challenge or a trigger, I often react instinctively, drawing on past experiences and memories that are stored in my hippocampus.

Choosing What to Absorb:

But this also means that I have a choice. I have the power to change the information I take in. If I want my intellect to be sharp, my emotional responses to be balanced, I need to be mindful of the information I allow to shape my thinking. The people I surround myself with, the media I consume, the conversations I engage in, all of these things fill up that vault. If I choose to fill it with positivity, wisdom, and healthy perspectives, I'm not only enhancing my intellect, but I'm also cultivating emotional responses that are aligned with peace, love, and understanding.

I can take charge of what enters my mind and, in turn, influence my emotional health and my reactions to the world. My hippocampus doesn't have to store the burdens of past trauma or negativity. Instead, I can consciously choose to fill it with nurturing thoughts, empowering experiences, and moments of clarity that will support my growth, peace, and inner strength. It's in this awareness that I begin to realize just how much control I have over my own mental and emotional landscape.

Morning Mindfulness:

The impact of the information we consume first thing in the morning is more powerful than we realize. It's as if our minds are an empty canvas, waiting to be filled, and whatever we paint on that canvas during the first moments of our day stays with us and shapes the energy we carry forward. I've noticed that the news we often read in the morning is filled with distressing and upsetting stories, bomb blasts, accidents, violence, things that can instantly shift our mindset to a place of fear, anxiety, and negativity.

For example, when I wake up and read about some tragic event, I start my day already feeling anxious, as if the weight of the world has been placed on my shoulders. Then, when my child is late, my mind jumps to the worst-case scenario: "What if something happened to them?" That automatic leap into anxiety feels so out of my control, but in truth, it's rooted in the constant negative stimuli I've allowed myself to absorb. The moment I open my eyes, my energy is at its peak, and yet, it's often consumed by distressing news.

I've come to realize that I don't have to let the external world dictate how I feel when I first wake up. The truth is, the beginning of my day offers me the opportunity to choose what I want to fill my mind with. Meditation, yoga, and Pranayama offer me a way to center myself, to connect with the stillness within me, and to fill my mind with peace and calmness before anything else. If I could change the habit of reaching for the newspaper and instead reach for something that nurtures my mind and soul, whether that's a deep breath, a mindful moment of gratitude, or a few minutes of meditation, I would change the course of my entire day.

I have the power to be mindful of the energy I consume, and by filling my morning with practices that bring me peace and clarity, I set the tone for the rest of the day. I'm beginning to understand just how important it is to protect my mental and emotional space, especially in those precious first moments of the morning. I owe it to myself to create a positive, grounded start to my day so that I can respond to the world with calm and resilience, instead of reacting with fear or anxiety. It's a small but profound shift that can transform how I experience life.

The Illusion of Blame:

It's painful to realize that I spent so much of my life believing that my emotions, my happiness, and my state of mind were all dependent on what was happening outside of me. I blamed others, I blamed situations, thinking that if they were different, I would feel better, be happier, at peace. I lived under the illusion that my emotions were always someone else's fault. And so, I waited, often in frustration and anxiety, for people to change, for circumstances to align, thinking that would be the key to my happiness.

In those moments, I didn't see how disempowering that belief was. I didn't realize that by blaming others and waiting for the world to change, I was handing over the reins of my emotional well-being to external forces over which I had no control. The truth is, this made me feel small, helpless, like a victim of life. I felt like I was constantly at the mercy of things outside my control, waiting for them to shift so I could feel happy. But in reality, I was stuck in a cycle, unable to break free.

Creating Internal Harmony:

When I finally started to see the truth that my thoughts and feelings were not dictated by others, but rather by how I was choosing to respond to them, that was a turning point. I realized that I have the power to choose my thoughts, my reactions, and my emotional state. I began to understand that the energy I give to situations, people, and circumstances is what ultimately shapes how I feel. When I choose to respond with love, understanding, and calm, I can change my internal world, regardless of what's happening around me.

It was an incredibly freeing realization. I no longer needed to wait for the world to change or for others to behave differently to feel at peace. I could create my own peace, my own happiness, from within. It's a beautiful thing to feel empowered, to know that I hold the key to my emotional state, and I no longer have to live as a victim of circumstance. I am the creator of my emotions, and I am learning to take responsibility for how I feel, knowing that I have the power to change it.

CHAPTER 8

APPROVAL, ACCEPTANCE, APPRECIATION

The Illusion of External Happiness:

For so long, I sought my happiness outside of myself, relying on the approval, acceptance, and appreciation of others. I became addicted to these three A's, believing that my worth, my value, and my happiness depended on how others perceived me. I shaped my life around what others thought of me, choosing paths that they would approve of, even if it meant compromising my own values and integrity. I lost myself in that pursuit.

Living in Fear:

I didn't see it at the time, but in doing this, I was living in constant fear. What if I failed to meet expectations? What if they didn't appreciate me? What if I wasn't accepted? My happiness was on a fragile pedestal, depending entirely on the behavior and opinions of others, and I was always at the mercy of that. I had no control.

Instead of creating genuine joy, I kept creating emotions of fear, anxiety, hurt, and jealousy. I was caught in a web of emotions that ultimately took me further away from the peace I longed for.

Looking in the Wrong Places:

I thought I could find happiness at the end of a goal, in the achievement of success. I believed that success would fill my heart with joy. But in reality, even when I achieved what I thought I wanted, it was never enough. I was left empty, still searching for that elusive feeling. I looked for happiness in accomplishments, in material possessions, in relationships, thinking that once I had them, I'd finally be at peace.

But the truth is happiness isn't something that can be found outside of us. I had forgotten that happiness is not a destination—it is a value, a state of being that's already within me. All along, I had been looking in the wrong places, neglecting the fact that the source of true happiness is my own sense of self-worth.

Liberation Through Self-Connection:

This realization is both liberating and painful. To think that I spent so much of my life chasing something I already had inside me, brings a deep sense of sorrow, but also hope: the hope that I can now shift my focus inward and reconnect with the happiness that's always been there, waiting to be acknowledged. It's a reminder that I don't need to depend on external validation to feel good about who I am. I am enough, just as I am, and my happiness comes from within.

CHAPTER 9

SELF-RESPECT

Nurturing the True Self:

Taking care of myself means nurturing the essence of who I truly am, honoring my values and remembering my worth. It's about being in a state of self-respect, which is so different from ego. Self-respect doesn't come from external validation or achievements. It comes from an inner connection with my true self, my soul, and the values that lie within me: love, peace, happiness, power, knowledge, humility, and bliss.

When I respect myself, I honor these qualities, and I realize that my true value can only be known by me deep within. This is self-esteem, not based on what others think or do, but grounded in the unwavering truth of who I am.

The soul is pure, made up of original sanskaras, the essence of my being. But over time, I have gathered acquired sanskaras, influenced by the world around me. True self-respect is when I reconnect with my original state, untouched by the judgments or behaviors of others. It's about being so deeply rooted in my own truth that, regardless of what happens around me, I choose peace.

Choosing Calm Amidst Chaos:

When I am in a state of self-respect, I do not let external circumstances shake my calm. I accept others with all their imperfections, knowing that they are also navigating their own journey. It's so easy to get caught in the chaos of others' actions and words, to react emotionally, but when I am rooted in self-respect, I feel no need to react or judge.

Judgment Blocks Respect:

Every time I feel myself fluctuating, when I feel hurt by someone's words, or when I am swayed by external situations, I know that self-respect is slipping away. And in that moment, I remind myself: respect for myself comes when I choose to remain calm, when I don't allow judgment to take hold. When there is pain, love is absent. And when I judge, respect is blocked.

So, I must always remember to reconnect with my inner peace and self-worth, no matter what's happening around me. I must learn to rise above the noise, and in that stillness, I will find true love, true respect, and the deep sense of self that I've always been worthy of.

Beyond Labels:

The reason I fluctuate emotionally, mentally, and spiritually, is that I sometimes forget my true identity. It's easy to get lost in the labels that others place upon me. "You're lazy," "You're slow," "You're untrustworthy." But these labels aren't truly who I am. They come from the perceptions and filters of others, shaped by their own experiences and acquired sanskaras. They don't reflect the essence of who I really am.

At my core, I am pure. I am trustworthy. I am capable. If I can remember this truth, I won't be swayed by the judgments of others. When I know my true identity, I can remain steady and calm, even when others react in ways that don't align with my values. And in that calmness, I create a space for self-respect.

Calmness as Influence:

A calm mind is powerful. It has the ability to influence the unstable minds around it. If I know I am a soul of pure intentions and values, I can see that the person before me is also a soul at their core, even if their actions don't reflect it. So instead of reacting with anger, disappointment, or frustration, I can send out energy of acceptance and understanding. When I accept others' behavior without judgment, I'm influencing them, not by force, but by radiating love and understanding. Acceptance means love.

But when I forget who I truly am, I start seeking respect from others. If my respect depends on external validation, then I'm caught in an endless cycle. If people behave as I want them to, I feel respected. If they don't, I feel disrespected. My emotions become a roller coaster, swinging with every external change. So, where does my true self come into play in all this?

Internal vs. External Validation:

True respect comes from within. It's grounded in my values. When I respect myself, I don't need to seek respect from others. I don't need to be validated externally because I already know my worth. And when I respect myself, that respect naturally flows to others. The more I honor my values, the more I respect others for their unique journey and experiences.

Creating Respect Within:

When I am weak, when I forget my inner strength, I depend on others to fill that void, to make me feel good about myself. But the truth is, if I truly want respect, I must first create it within myself. Respect isn't something I can demand or expect from others. It's something I must radiate from within.

And when I respect myself deeply, when I create a life rooted in my values, respect will come to me effortlessly. It will radiate from me like light, and it will attract more respect from the universe.

Respect is not something I seek, it is something I embody, and by embodying it, I receive it back tenfold.

This is the ultimate truth: by respecting myself, I create respect. By knowing my true value, I never have to chase it again. It will always be with me, and it will always flow outward into every relationship, every interaction, and every moment.

EGO

From Soul to Body:

The first connection of the soul is with the body. The soul identifies with the body, its roles, name, status, and possessions. This attachment creates ego. "I am this body, I am this role." Whenever we are attached to something we tend to become heavy.

The Birth of Ego:

Ego is a heavy burden that we carry, an attachment to a false image of ourselves. It creates a separation between who we truly are and who we think we should be. For so long, I defined myself by the labels and roles I've accumulated over time, each one a piece of my identity, but not the whole truth. I am a woman, a daughter, a friend, a wife, a mother, a doctor, and so many other things. But these labels aren't who I truly am. They are just the roles I play, the masks I wear.

When Roles Define Worth:

When I attached "I" to these labels, I began to lose sight of my true self. My identity became fluid, changing depending on the people I was with and the situations I was in. With some, I felt superior, with others, inferior. I let these roles define my worth. I became consumed by them, thinking that I was only valuable if I fulfilled these roles perfectly.

Defending the False Self:

But when I identified so strongly with these labels, I created space for ego to grow. The moment my son didn't listen to me or someone spoke ill of my family, my heart would swell with offense, with insult. I was no longer calm or centered in my true being, I became reactive. I would respond with criticism, loudness, control because I thought I was defending my "identity." But in reality, I was only defending the false self that I had created.

Remembering the True Self:

My true self is not bound by labels or roles. My true self is pure, lovable, peaceful, and filled with happiness. When I operate from the consciousness of these roles, I move further away from my essence. I become entangled in the fluctuations of my emotions, seeking validation, approval, and control. But when I remember who I really am, I can let go of the ego. I realize that my worth doesn't come from what I do or what others think of me. It comes from who I am at my core. An infinite, peaceful being.

And so, I begin the journey of letting go of the labels that have defined me for so long. I start to step into the truth of my soul, the truth that I am love, peace, and joy, not attached to any role or expectation. When I live from this place, I stop reacting, I stop defending, and I stop feeling the need to prove my worth. I simply am, and in that being, I find true freedom and fulfillment.

The Computer Analogy:

The analogy of a personal computer is so powerful when reflecting on the true nature of our being. Just like every computer comes pre-installed with basic programs, essential, universal elements that allow it to function, every soul is born with inherent qualities that are pure, loving, peaceful, and powerful. These qualities form the core of who we are. They are the value system we all share, the essence of our true self.

But as we journey through life, we start accumulating external files, our labels, roles, and experiences. We begin to define ourselves not by the purity of our soul, but by what we do, who we are to others, and how we are perceived in the world. These are the acquired traits, the external identities that shape how we see ourselves and others. And with these acquisitions, we begin to lose touch with who we truly are beneath it all.

The problem is that, like being stuck in a maze of files and folders on a computer, we forget that the root system, the foundation of who we are, is already built in. We get lost in the surface-level identities, the roles, the external validation, and forget that at our core, we are a peaceful soul, full of love, wisdom, and light.

Because we live in a world where we are so attached to body consciousness, we constantly look at ourselves and others through the lens of these external labels. That's why we fluctuate our responses to situations and people become driven by these labels. One moment we feel powerful because we are seen in a certain light, the next we feel small because we are criticized or overlooked. This constant ebb and flow of emotions is a result of identifying with the wrong thing, the external instead of the internal.

Choosing the Higher Identity:

But the truth is, beneath every label, every acquired trait, there is a pure, unchanging essence of who we are. When we remember this, we begin to operate from a place of stillness, not defined by the highs and lows of external approval or disapproval. We realize that our true self is not the sum of our roles and responsibilities but the soul that exists beyond all of that, filled with love, peace, and the quiet wisdom of knowing we are enough just as we are.

When we reconnect with that truth, we stop fluctuating. We can stand firm in the reality that we are not what we do or what we are labeled, but what we are at our very core, a soul of infinite value. And from that place, we can approach the world with calmness, acceptance, and a deep understanding that we are whole.

Declaring Your Truth:

The words "I AM" carry immense power, don't they? These two words are like seeds we plant in the soil of our soul. Whatever we choose to fill the blank space with is what we nurture, grow, and ultimately become. If I declare, "I AM a soul," I am aligning myself with the truth of my existence, pure, peaceful, loving, and full of light. I step into the consciousness of who I truly am, remembering that I am not my body, not my roles, not the labels society places on me. I am a being of love, a being of joy, a being of infinite worth.

And when I embody this truth, I radiate it outward into the world. What I create within me, I experience around me.

But if I identify with the body and attach to its emotions, its pain, its anger, then my "I AM" becomes shaped by these fleeting, external states. "I AM angry," "I AM hurt," "I AM sad" and suddenly, I find myself trapped in a cycle where I experience these emotions more and more. The universe, in its infinite wisdom, responds to the energy I put out. If I constantly declare negativity, the universe blesses me with more experiences to validate those feelings. I draw more anger, more sadness, more frustration into my life.

The power of "I AM" lies in its ability to shape our reality. What follows those words determines our mental state, our emotional state, and ultimately the energy we send into the universe. If I choose to affirm love, peace, happiness, and strength, then that's what I attract. I become more aligned with who I truly am, rather than what I think I am based on external circumstances.

In every moment, we have a choice. The words we speak to ourselves, the thoughts we entertain, they shape not just our present experience but our future too. So let's choose wisely. Let's choose the highest version of ourselves. Let's remember, "I AM" is not just a statement—it's a declaration of who we are in our essence, in our truth. And when we speak from that place, we open the door to a life of infinite possibilities, of love, of peace, of connection, and of deep, unconditional happiness.

Seeing Beyond Hierarchy:

When I'm role-conscious, I let external labels and societal positions dictate how I show up in the world. I might treat my driver with one level of respect, my receptionist with another, and my CEO with yet another, based on how I perceive them in the hierarchy of life. And this fluctuating behavior is not true to who I really am.

But what if I could forget these roles for a moment and remember my true self? What if, in each interaction, I could simply be the pure, loving, peaceful soul that I am, without attaching judgments to someone's position, appearance, or status? When I remember that I am neither superior nor inferior, when I am simply a soul interacting with another soul, my behaviuor becomes consistent. There is no judgment, no fluctuation, no comparison. I would treat my driver, my receptionist, my CEO, with the same respect, kindness, and understanding because, at the core, we are all the same. Souls on a journey, playing different roles.

This is the beauty of remembering our true identity: we stop identifying ourselves with the external circumstances, roles, or positions we hold. We realize that our value does not come from the titles we wear or the company we keep, but from the love, peace, and power within us. When we act from this space of true self-awareness, our behaviuor is aligned, grounded, and pure. We can offer the same respect, care, and attention to every person we meet, because we recognize that each soul is equally valuable.

It's only when we forget our true selves and get caught up in external labels that we start to behave in ways that fluctuate, sometimes out of insecurity, sometimes out of superiority. But when we choose to see others as equals, when we choose to embody love and respect for ourselves and for them, our interactions become harmonious, balanced, and true. And that is where our real self shines through.

ATTACHMENT:

Redefining Love and Attachment:

This analogy is so powerful because it truly shifts our understanding of love and attachment. We often hear that "love is attachment," but in reality, attachment can cause more harm than good. It's like tying ourselves to another person's pain and suffering, which only pulls us down further into the pit with them. We think that if we feel their pain deeply, that's love. But what if love is not about sinking into the same emotions they are feeling, but rather being strong and stable for them?

Imagine, if instead of attaching ourselves to their pain, we allowed ourselves to remain detached. Meaning not numb or indifferent, but calm and centered in our own sense of peace. From that place of stability, we could help them, guide them, and offer support without losing ourselves. In detachment, we don't allow their hurt to become our own. Instead, we can be the steady presence that lifts them up.

Mistaking shared pain for compassion:

True love isn't about becoming enmeshed in someone else's emotions to the point that we lose ourselves. It's about being able to hold space for them, to feel compassion and empathy, but to also remain rooted in our own sense of peace and strength. When we do this, we empower them to heal and rise, because we are not caught in the whirlwind of their suffering.

The Freedom of True Love:

This kind of love is freeing. It's unconditional, it's non-dependent, and it's grounded in the deepest sense of inner strength. When we are truly loving, we don't need to absorb the other person's pain. Instead, we can be a guiding light for them, showing them the way out of their struggles while remaining peaceful and intact within ourselves. This is the power of detachment, not from the person, but from the emotional turbulence that clouds our ability to help and support them in the most meaningful way.

Losing the Self in Attachment:

When we are attached to others in a way that causes us to lose ourselves in their pain, we end up not just sharing their burden but actually multiplying it. Attachment, in this sense, creates dependency, not just for the other person, but for ourselves as well. We depend on them to make us feel okay, to act in a certain way so we can feel in control, and when they don't, we react out of fear and pain.

Replacing fear and control with wisdom and grace:

But true love is never rooted in fear or attachment. Real love comes from a place of detachment, not in the sense of being indifferent or uncaring, but in being emotionally stable and strong enough to handle situations without being swept away by them. Detachment doesn't mean withdrawing or cutting off. It means that, no matter what the situation is, I stay grounded in my own peace, my own strength, and my own understanding of what truly matters.

If my child comes to me hurt, yes, my heart breaks for them, but I do not allow their pain to become my pain. I do not lose myself in the emotions of the moment. Instead, I can offer them comfort and strength because I am steady within myself. I can approach the situation with love, calmness, and clarity, and that energy will help them heal as well. Reacting with anger or fear only compounds the problem. But responding with love and calm intention creates space for resolution.

Responding with clarity, not chaos:

The power of detachment lies in our ability to handle challenges with wisdom and grace, rather than becoming entangled in the emotions of the situation. When we can respond to a situation from a place of inner strength, we not only help others in the most constructive way but we also model how to approach life's challenges with maturity this is the true strength. The ability to remain calm and centered, regardless of external circumstances. This is where love truly thrives.

Attachment is about pain; detachment is about empowerment

Releasing the Knots:

The Knots of Emotional Baggage:

The image of the entangled rope is a powerful one, and it beautifully reflects how emotional baggage builds up in our lives. We unknowingly create these knots in our hearts when we hold on to past hurts, grudges, or unresolved feelings. At first, it may seem like something small, but as time goes on, the emotional strain only grows tighter. Just as the rope becomes more painful and restricted, our hearts become heavy and constricted with these unresolved emotions.

Entangled Within Our Own Emotions:

The pain and inflammation vividly reflect how our emotional wounds affect our well-being. Just as the flow of oxygen is cut off when we hold onto negativity, we cut off our ability to experience love, peace, and joy. We find ourselves disconnected, and that emotional "oxygen" we need to thrive becomes scarce.

Untangling the Knots Within:

But the most beautiful truth is that, just like the rope, once we untangle these knots, through forgiveness, letting go, and healing, there is a smooth, uninterrupted flow. When we release what no longer serves us, we allow ourselves to be free, to breathe deeply, and to embrace life fully again. Our hearts become open, our minds clear, and we can truly experience the love and peace that were always within us.

It's in this gentle, patient unraveling that we come back to who we truly are, unbound, untangled, and whole. And in that space, there is infinite peace.

The Invisible Threads Between Souls:

Every relationship, whether it's with a family member, a friend, or even a colleague, carries the weight of our shared emotions. The knots we've tied over time, sometimes without even realizing it. These emotional knots can be from past experiences, misunderstandings, unhealed wounds, or even things passed down through generations. The more we interact with each other, the more we build on these knots, creating a tangled web of unresolved emotions that manifest as pain, frustration, and even heartache.

The Karma of Connection:

The pain we feel in relationships is often a signal to us. It's a message urging us to pause, reflect, and make a conscious choice. To heal, to let go, to forgive, to release the old patterns. In every interaction, we are shaping our karmic exchange, and we have the power to choose a different path, to break the cycle of hurt and pain.

Breaking the Cycle of Pain:

Letting go of emotional hurt can feel like an impossible task, especially when you're deeply connected to the pain that others have caused. But when you start accepting others' sanskars (their unique patterns of behavior, beliefs, and emotional responses), it opens up a space for healing. You begin to see that their actions are shaped by their own wounds, fears, and experiences, which might have nothing to do with you personally.

Acceptance vs. Endurance: The True Meaning of Letting Go:

Acceptance doesn't mean excusing or tolerating hurtful behavior, but rather releasing the emotional grip it has on you. It's about understanding that everyone is on their own journey, and sometimes, the pain they cause stems from their own struggles and unhealed wounds.

Healing Through Compassion and Perspective:

When you let go of judgment and embrace compassion, both for them and for yourself, you free yourself from the constant weight of emotional hurt. You no longer need to carry their burdens as your own. You start to heal, not by changing others, but by changing your perspective on their actions and accepting them as they are, without letting their actions define your worth or your peace.

Embracing the Journey—Yours and Theirs:

It's not an easy process, but it's one of the most freeing things you can do for your own heart. It's about choosing to release what no longer serves you, so you can make space for love, growth, and a deeper understanding of both yourself and others.

The Sacred Purpose of Our Relationships:

And yet, there's a beautiful truth hidden in this pattern. We are born and reborn into these relationships not to perpetuate the pain, but to untie the knots, to heal and clear the karmic imprints that have bound us. Every person we meet is a mirror, reflecting a part of ourselves that needs healing. Sometimes, the same souls come into our lives again and again because there is unfinished business, a lesson still to be learned, an emotion still to be healed. These repeated encounters are not accidents—they are opportunities for growth and transformation.

Healing the Karmic Knots of the Soul:

As we begin to untangle the knots, by understanding, accepting, and loving ourselves and others more deeply, we create a smoother, more peaceful flow in our relationships. We no longer see these souls as sources of pain but as the teachers they truly are. Each relationship, then, becomes an opportunity to clear our karmic accounts, to let go of what no longer serves us, and to step into a deeper connection, one based not on old wounds but on compassion, healing, and unconditional love.

From Karmic Bonds to Soul Freedom:

In this way, the cycle of birth and death becomes not a chain that keeps us trapped, but a process of profound growth, where we continuously evolve, learn, and rise above the pain. And ultimately, we free ourselves from the knots, finding peace and harmony in our relationships, in our hearts, and in our souls.

The Reflection and the Reality:

This reflection of the Banyan tree in the water holds such deep significance. The tree itself represents our spiritual essence, the eternal soul, while its reflection in the water symbolizes our material existence, the world we experience through desires and attachments. Just as the reflection is never the true form, this material world is not our true home; it's a place where we often get caught in the illusion of what we see and feel. Our true home is the spiritual world, a realm of peace, serenity, and tranquility, where there are no desires to bind us.

Homecoming: Beyond the Cycles of Desire and Attachment:

When we talk about the "Dukhalaya" or the place of misery, it resonates deeply with the understanding that our physical existence, though beautiful, is often riddled with pain and suffering due to our desires, attachments, and the cycles of birth and death. These are the knots that keep us bound here. The journey of life is essentially a journey of untying these knots, of releasing the burdens of ego, attachment, and desire, and returning to the peace that is our true nature.

The Moment of Liberation:

When we finally begin to untie the emotional and spiritual knots, when we let go of all the things that tie us to this material world, like grudges, fears, and attachments, that is the moment we begin to experience true freedom. That is the moment of Moksha, liberation from the cycles of birth and death. It is not about physical death, but the death of the ego, the death of all that keeps us from experiencing our true selves. In that stillness, we reconnect with the purity of our soul, and we find the peace that we are always meant to experience.

From Attachment to Awakening:

In the meantime, this journey of untying the knots requires us to practice compassion, forgiveness, and acceptance, towards ourselves and others. When we do this, we start to dissolve the barriers we have built and create a smoother path back to the spiritual world. It is about cooperation, understanding, and love. It's about seeing beyond the reflections and understanding that every soul we meet is just another reflection of the divine, another opportunity for healing and growth.

Ultimately, the purpose of this life is to return to that state of pure peace, free from the entanglements of the material world, where we can finally experience the bliss of our true home.

CHAPTER 10

CONTROL

This illusion of control over others is so deeply ingrained in us that we often don't even realize the extent to which it shapes our interactions and relationships. We've been conditioned to believe that by expressing anger, hurt, or frustration, we can force people to change their behavior to fit our expectations. The belief that controlling others, through emotional manipulation or subtle pressure, can create harmony or a sense of order in our lives is so misleading.

The Trap of Conditional Love:

But in reality, it only leads to deeper insecurities and unmet needs. As children, we were taught that when we did things the "right" way, according to others' standards, we would receive love and validation. Parents, teachers, and others around us often showed approval or disapproval based on our actions, making us believe that their love was conditional, tied to our behavior and achievements. This led us to grow up thinking that love, acceptance, and respect from others were based on what we could do for them, rather than simply who we are.

The Cycle of External Validation:

This pattern creates a cycle of dependency. We constantly seek external validation, constantly try to "perform" to win love and approval, but the deeper truth is that real love cannot be earned or controlled, it must be unconditional. True love, the love that we all long for, comes from within. It is a love for ourselves, rooted in self-acceptance, which then allows us to love others without trying to control or manipulate them. When we let go of the need to control how others act, we can experience a freedom that comes with unconditional love and acceptance, not only from others, but from ourselves as well.

Turning Inward:

When we shift our focus from controlling others to nurturing ourselves, we realize that the love we seek outside has always been inside us. The moment we stop trying to change or control others to make ourselves feel loved, we open the door to deeper, more genuine connections, based on mutual respect and understanding. Our relationships transform when we let go of the need to control and simply allow people to be who they are, accepting them as they are, without trying to mold them into something they're not.

The Power of Allowing

This is where true love and peace begin, when we stop seeking approval and start offering love freely, without conditions or expectations. It is in this space of acceptance and peace that we find ourselves truly at ease, free from the constant need to control and manipulate, and able to experience love in its purest, most transformative form.

The Roots of Control

The need to control others often comes from a place of deep insecurity and fear. When someone tries to control, it's as though they are trying to protect themselves from the vulnerability of the unknown, from the fear that they might not have everything under their command. They may feel powerless inside, so they try to assert power over others to convince themselves that they have control over their lives.

However, true strength doesn't come from controlling people or situations. It comes from understanding that we are not in control of everything, and that's okay. The desire to control stems from a belief that we must always have everything in order, that we must always be in charge, but that belief only creates stress and fear: fear of losing control, and fear of what might happen if things don't go the way we expect.

The Fear Behind Control

When we try to control, we often don't realize that we are creating an environment of fear, not only for the other person but also for ourselves. The person being controlled starts to feel helpless, trapped by the idea that they don't have a choice. But the truth is, we always have a choice, even in those moments when we feel manipulated or controlled. By acknowledging that we are choosing to be in that situation, we regain a sense of power and autonomy.

Reclaiming Our Inner Power:

This shift in perspective is so powerful because it frees us from the illusion of powerlessness. We may not always be able to control the actions of others, but we always have control over how we respond, over how we navigate situations. Choosing to recognize that every action is a choice, and understanding that we are the ones who decide how we react, restores our inner strength and dignity.

We can't force others to change, nor should we try to control them. But by letting go of the need to control, we embrace a deeper sense of freedom. True power comes from knowing that we can stand firm in who we are, make conscious choices, and let go of the fear that others can dictate our lives.

The Victim Trap:

In situations like this, when our boss is shouting or trying to control us, it's easy to fall into the trap of feeling like a victim. We often blame the boss, the situation, or even ourselves for being stuck. But the truth is, we always have a choice, even if it doesn't seem like one at first.

When we acknowledge that we are choosing to stay in the job because we need it for our family, or because we don't have another option at the moment, we shift the entire dynamic. We stop seeing ourselves as powerless, as though life is happening to us. Instead, we recognize that we are making a choice, even if that choice is to endure the situation for a larger reason.

Shifting from Powerlessness to Empowerment:

This shift in perspective is deeply empowering because it allows us to stop blaming others and the world around us. We take back control of our emotional response and our actions. We stop feeling like a victim of the circumstances and recognize that we are in charge of how we choose to react. And when we accept responsibility for that choice, we reclaim our self-respect and our dignity.

The Weight of Expectation:

When our sense of power is dependent on others listening to us, we unknowingly place our happiness and emotional well-being in their hands. It's not easy, of course. There will be moments when the pressure feels overwhelming, and the need for validation or approval from others can feel consuming. But when we remind ourselves that everything we do is a choice, whether it's to stay, to speak up, to stay silent, or to leave, it gives us a sense of ownership over our lives. We don't have to give away our peace and power just because someone else is shouting or trying to control us. The moment we own our choice, we step into our true strength.

In that space of awareness, we realize that we don't need to react with frustration or anger. We can choose to remain calm, centered, and respectful of ourselves and others. We no longer give our power away to the external situation. We are not victims; we are the architects of our own lives.

Owning Our Power:

By consciously choosing, we stay in a state of self-respect, which is the highest form of inner strength. The more we remember that our reactions are within our control, the less we will be at the mercy of others' behavior. This is how we cultivate true power. By honoring ourselves, accepting our circumstances, and knowing that we are always in control of how we respond, even when we can't control what happens around us.

It creates a fragile illusion of control that crumbles the moment they choose to act or respond differently. The truth is, we can never fully control how others behave. Every person has their own free will, their own mind, and their own way of processing the world around them.

The Fragility of External Validation:

When we tie our power to external validation, such as someone listening to us, we create a false sense of security that is vulnerable to the unpredictability of life. This attachment to control creates a deep sense of resistance and frustration whenever things don't go as planned or people don't behave as we hope they will. We begin to feel that we're not being heard, that we're not being respected, and that our power is slipping away. This leads to an internal conflict, as we battle between the desire to feel heard and the reality that others have their own thoughts and choices.

The Ripple Effect of Resistance:

When we send out resistance, we are unknowingly creating a ripple of negative energy that comes back to us, affecting both ourselves and others. This cycle of resistance only builds walls between us and the people around us. It creates an atmosphere of judgment, where we begin to see the other person as wrong, and in return, they may begin to see us as wrong as well. This cycle of negative energy only depletes us emotionally, creating division and pain in our relationships.

The Essence of True Leadership:

In contrast, a leader understands that every person comes from a place of his or her own experiences, beliefs, and emotions. A leader doesn't need to control or dictate; instead, he or she leads with understanding, empathy, and acceptance. He or she understands that everyone has a unique viewpoint, and he or she respects that without judgment. By doing this, a leader remains calm, grounded, and compassionate, which, in turn, influences the people around him or her in a positive way.

Seeing Through the Lens of Compassion:

When we accept others for who they are, when we recognize their perspectives and appreciate them for the unique individuals they are, we not only create harmony but also respect ourselves. Acceptance is a powerful act of self-respect because it means we are not getting caught up in the judgments of the mind or allowing them to dictate how we feel. We are choosing to remain calm, regardless of the behavior of others, which allows us to stand in our true power.

Influence Over Control:

So if I want him to change, I need to remain calm in my head. This will send him the energy of acceptance. In this way, I will be able to INFLUENCE the person.

What are the steps that I should follow so that the right energy is created?

If I am making mistakes, it means I have depleted my energy and I do not have positive energy. We are all attached to our various labels of how things should be. To be in a state of self-respect, we need to engage in self-talk.

1. When others don't act according to what we feel is right, the first self-talk we need to engage in is that the other person is right. How can the other person be right? Imagine someone is angry and is shouting. Is he right? Yes, he is right. If a person is repeatedly doing something, he forms his sanskar. If a situation arises and if he gets angry, he is right because that is what he

knows and is seeing the situation through that lens. Conflict begins when we start labeling the other person as wrong.

2. The second self-talk we need to engage in is that everyone is making their own choices. I understand them. Nobody would deliberately try to do the wrong thing. At that moment they felt that was the best decision to make. So we need to respect others for the choices they make.
3. I respect myself by remaining calm. Is it necessary to spoil my karma because of someone else's karma? We normally react because we are attached to the images of how the scene should be. With every negative reaction, I am going to deplete my energy. I NEED PROFIT. I cannot afford to lose all the positive energy that I have created. When I stay calm, I stay connected with my true self and I respect myself for my value system.
4. I know myself. If I know myself truly then I don't need to keep fluctuating on what people are saying about me. People say according to their belief system and Sanskars. If someone has worn pink glasses he will see everything pink. They are not saying this to me but this is their nature and they feel this way for everyone.
5. The biggest truth is the LAW OF KARMA. What I give, I receive back. If someone is ill-treating me, let me tell myself, I have just received something I had given earlier. Then there should not be any question raised – why is this happening to me? The right thing to do is to first ask forgiveness for sending the negative energy to the other person earlier. Then to understand that the other person had consumed the negative energy and has sent it back. But today I choose to end this negative karmic exchange and pray to God to give him an abundance of positive energy that will enable him to make good choices. This is called TRANSFORMING ENERGY. I have just transformed negative energy to positive energy. Since I did not create negative thoughts, I increased my internal power and I was energized. The more powerful you become, the less other people's behavior affects you.

Clarity in Stillness:

When I remain stable within myself, my calmness radiates outward, and it has the power to influence those around me. My inner stability is a gift, not just to myself, but to others as well. It creates a space where I can see things clearly, without the clouded judgments or frustrations that often come with emotional turbulence. In that space of stillness, I can offer my opinion, my guidance, without attachment to how it is received.

Speaking Like a Master:

Giving my opinion like a master means offering wisdom with clarity, yet accepting that others may not choose to listen or take it. This is not about control. It's about sharing what I believe is beneficial with a sense of detachment. I do not need them to act on it, and I do not need to be hurt or offended if they do not. I have no power over their choices. But I do have power over my response, and by choosing not to react, I preserve my peace.

When I offer advice, I must ask myself: Is this for their good, or am I seeking validation or comfort from them? If my intentions are pure, the energy behind my words will be genuine, and it will resonate with them. It's not about winning them over or getting them to agree with me. It's about offering something that may help them, free of ego and judgment. When the intention behind my advice is truly selfless, the person receiving it will feel that energy and will be more open to listening and changing.

Purity of Intention:

The beauty lies in detachment. I offer my thoughts, but I do not attach my happiness or worth to whether they are received. People are free to choose how they respond, and when I accept that truth, I release myself from unnecessary emotional strain. And in this freedom, both the person and I are empowered to be our true selves. Detachment means letting go of the images that we have created of how people and situations should be. This is true power, true happiness.

Criticism:

The Ripple Effect of Criticism:

When someone criticizes, it's as though they are pouring negativity into the atmosphere, creating ripples of anger, resentment, and frustration. It's easy to forget that in that moment, they are not only judging the other person but also distorting their own peace. Criticism stems from an attachment to the belief that one's view of right and wrong is the only valid perspective, and the need to correct others becomes an unhealthy obsession.

What happens when we criticize is that we lose the ability to see the person in front of us clearly. We focus so much on their faults, their supposed shortcomings, that we become blind to their potential, to their goodness, to their humanity. When we criticize, we block love because love cannot coexist with judgment. Criticism pushes us further from understanding and compassion. It brings only division and distance.

The Cost of Criticism:

At that moment, I am no longer acting out of kindness, understanding, or patience. I am not seeing the person as they are, with all their complexity, struggles, and inherent value. Instead, I am seeing them only as a target for my opinions, which may or may not be accurate or helpful. What does that do to me? It drains me. It hardens my heart and closes me off to the possibilities of growth and connection.

Beyond Right and Wrong:

When we criticize, we are so attached to the idea of what's right and wrong, of how things should be, that we forget about the space between the "shoulds" and the "is." In that space, there is room for acceptance, understanding, and, ultimately, growth. Not just in the person we are criticizing, but in ourselves.

Disconnecting Through Judgment:

And so, it becomes important to ask ourselves: How often do I criticize others in a day? How many times do I judge their actions, their choices, and their behaviors? When I judge, I am disconnecting from them and from my own higher self. When I criticize, I am forgetting my ability to love unconditionally, to accept people as they are, with all their imperfections. I am choosing to create distance instead of connection.

And so, I ask myself: What would it look like to stop criticizing? What would it feel like to accept, to understand, and to love instead? To approach others not with a need to correct them, but with the willingness to see them for who they truly are—the same way I long to be seen, heard, and understood. Because in that space of love and acceptance, I find my true power.

The Hidden Pain of Criticism:

When we witness someone being criticized, it's natural to feel empathy, to feel sorry for the person who is being hurt. We feel their pain, their vulnerability, and wish for the judgment to stop. But in truth, the one who is criticizing is the one most in need of compassion, because criticism doesn't only hurt the other, it harms the one who creates it too.

The critic is not just transferring negative energy onto the person. they target; they are first absorbing it within themself. The anger, resentment, frustration, and judgment they release into the world are energies they feel deeply within. And it is only when these negative emotions are expressed that they pass them onto the other person

Negative Energy: A Two-Way Cycle:

This cycle of negativity leaves both the critic and the criticized in a web of pain, where no one truly wins. The one criticizing believes they are pointing out the wrong in another, but what they don't realize is that they are also revealing the hurt within themselves. In the end, both are suffering, one through the words spoken, and the other through the energy received. And the deepest truth is this: the person who criticizes is the one most in need of healing.

This is why we must remember: "Give what you need." If we need peace, we must give peace. If we need love, we must give love. If we need understanding, we must offer understanding. For when we give, we receive, not just from others, but from the universe itself. The energy we send out doesn't just go to the other; it's mirrored back to us, amplified.

Critic vs. Critical:

When we think of criticism, we need to reflect on the energy behind the words we speak. **Critic** and **Critical** may seem similar, but they come from different places. A **critic** offers feedback, focusing on actions, tasks, or work itself, pointing out what was done well and what could be improved. This form of critique is neutral. It speaks to the task at hand and allows room for growth. However, when we become **critical,** it's no longer about the task. It's about the **person**, the individual behind the work. It's no longer feedback, but judgment.

When we criticize the **work,** we allow the person to learn and grow. When we criticize the **person**, we diminish their spirit. The energy we carry when being critical is charged with judgment, and it hits the person, not their actions, but their worth. Imagine a film critic who reviews a film's content and quality, offering constructive criticism about a scene or a character. Now, imagine that same critic attacking the actor personally, saying they are not talented or capable. The difference is huge. One focuses on the work, and the other questions the very being of the person.

The same happens when we criticize someone close to us, especially our loved ones. Take the example of a parent criticizing their child. Instead of guiding the child to improve their actions, the parent's words focus on the child's character, calling them lazy, careless, or not good enough. This kind of criticism doesn't help the child grow. It makes them feel small, insignificant, and incapable of being anything more. It's like a delicate plant, trying to grow in a garden, having someone come along and trample it underfoot. The plant is not allowed to flourish because of the harshness and the force.

The Erosion of Self-Esteem:

Criticism that targets the person's character, rather than their actions, can leave lasting scars. It's painful and unnecessary. The child begins to feel as though they are not worthy of love, and they carry this self-doubt with them. Their self-esteem shrinks with every critical word, and they start to believe the judgment passed on them.

As humans, we all have the potential to grow, to bloom, to evolve. But when we are criticized, especially in a way that targets our worth as a person, it feels like we're being suffocated. We forget that we are not our mistakes. We are not the errors we make. We are not the flaws others see in us. But when we constantly hear that we are not enough or not good enough, it's hard to remember our worth.

Criticism, when focused on improvement, is a gift. Let us choose to be kind, nurturing critics, giving others the space to grow and be their true selves without fear of judgment.

Being Assertive:

Being a **critic** means recognizing that actions and people are separate. It's about assessing the **work** or **task** and offering feedback based on its quality, not on the character of the person behind it.

When we are **assertive**, we remain clear and strong in our own understanding, yet we respect the other person's dignity. Instead of saying, "You are wrong," we say, "This action can be improved." We direct our feedback towards the **act** and not the **person.** This shift in perspective makes a huge difference in how the message is received.

When we separate the deed from the doer, we create a space where people can be accountable for their actions without feeling as if their entire being is under scrutiny. So, let's be critics, but also be kind in our critiques. Let's be assertive, clear, and focused on the work, not the person. This is how we build each other up, how we inspire growth, and how we create an atmosphere of mutual respect and positive change.

Staying Present When Receiving Criticism:

When receiving criticism, the first step is to **stay in the present moment.** If we focus on what's being criticized rather than taking it personally, we can approach the situation with a clear mind. It's about **solution-focused thinking**, how can we move forward, improve, and learn from this moment? When we remain grounded in the now, we don't let the past define us or derail our confidence. The past is not in our control, but the present is. So, **stay present** and **take action.**

The Power of Words in Giving Feedback:

And when we give criticism to others, it's also important to remember that our words have the power to uplift or tear down. Instead of diving directly into what needs to be fixed, we should first **acknowledge the strengths** and **good work** that the person has done. By doing this, we **empower** them, making them feel valued and **respected.** Appreciation raises their self-esteem, and that positive energy makes them more open to constructive feedback.

Once we've established a sense of support, we can briefly address what needs to be improved and offer a clear solution. But here's the key: **once it's said, let it go.** Don't dwell on it, don't revisit it. Give them the space to process, execute, and grow. People thrive when they feel trusted and supported, not criticized endlessly. By releasing the need to keep reminding them, we allow them to feel empowered to take action.

Avoiding Self-Criticism:

Now, when we receive criticism, it's so easy to become self-critical. We may feel small or inadequate. Yes, the criticism may sting, but it's **the task** or the **action** that needs to be improved, not who we are as a person.

We can't run away from ourselves. We are with ourselves every moment. So, instead of internalizing the criticism, we can use it as an opportunity for growth. It's natural to feel defensive or hurt, but once we separate ourselves from the feedback, we can start to see it as a tool to improve, not as an indictment of our worth.

The Practice of Self-Love:

Ultimately, self-love is about accepting ourselves even when we don't meet the ideal. Instead of retreating into self-doubt, we can use each piece of feedback as a stepping stone to become better. The journey is about progress, not perfection. And by focusing on solutions, embracing positive energy, and not internalizing the criticism, we become stronger, kinder, and more confident in who we are, our flaws and all.

HOW TO TRANSFORM NEGATIVE ENERGY.

When we absorb negative energy, it feels like a heavy weight that drains us. It saps our strength and leaves us feeling exhausted, depleted. But the truth is, we **don't have to absorb that energy.** We don't have to let it define us or make us feel small. Instead, we have the **power** to **transform** it.

Self-Talk as a Shield:

Self-talk is a beautiful tool that we often overlook. In moments when criticism or negative energy comes our way, we can **pause** and remind ourselves: *"I know who I am. I am a powerful soul, full of love, peace, and wisdom. I understand my worth, and that's not something anyone can take away from me."* We need to anchor ourselves in our **true essence**, in the knowledge that we are not defined by the opinions or judgments of others. Others may not fully understand us, and that's okay. Their perspective is shaped by their own life experiences, their own filters. But **I know myself** and I know my potential.

We don't need to internalize their negative energy. Instead, we can **acknowledge** that what they say or do may come from their own wounds, their own fears, or past experiences. Their criticism or judgment is **not about us**. It's about their **sanskaras**, their beliefs, and their projections.

When we respond from a place of stability and understanding, it has the potential to be a **healing presence** for the other person. Imagine this: when someone criticizes us, if we remain grounded and calm, our energy can **soothe** their own inner struggles. It's like offering them a mirror that reflects their own potential for peace and growth, even if they can't see it in themselves yet.

Choosing Compassion Over Reaction:

So, rather than reacting with anger or hurt, we can choose to be compassionate. We are compassionate toward them because we understand that their behavior is a reflection of their journey. And in that moment, we honor our true selves and choose to let go of what's not ours to carry.

This healing energy doesn't just benefit them but it **protects us** from being depleted. The more we remember our true nature, the more we embody love, power, and inner peace. We can transform negative energy and use it to strengthen our own foundation, so we can rise above and continue to shine brightly, no matter what comes our way.

Happiness isn't something we can find in material things or external circumstances. It's a quiet, peaceful feeling that arises when we embrace contentment, which is deeply rooted in acceptance. True happiness is found when we accept ourselves for who we truly are, not in the perfection we try to portray or the expectations we put on ourselves. And it's the same with others. When we accept them for who they are, even in their imperfections, it brings peace to our hearts.

We have all encountered people whose actions or behaviors don't align with our expectations. We may feel irritated, hurt, or confused by them. But **realizing that everyone is shaped by their unique sanskars**, the collection of experiences and beliefs that make them who they are, helps us release judgment. We don't have the power to change them, nor should we try to. Instead, we can choose to accept them as they are, with love and compassion.

Acceptance Without Resignation:

Acceptance doesn't mean condoning bad behavior or resigning ourselves to being passive. It means understanding that **everyone is on their own journey**. When we accept someone's sanskars, especially the ones that are uncomfortable for us, we free ourselves from the burden of resistance. We stop trying to change them, and instead, we give ourselves the space to remain calm and **unshaken** in the face of their actions.

When someone acts with anger, criticism, hurt, or resentment, we may be tempted to react, but it's important to remember that this is **their truth,** not ours. Their anger doesn't have to become our anger. Their hurt doesn't need to become our hurt. We can allow their feelings to be valid for them, while choosing to **hold our peace.**

Real change can only come from within. And when we accept others' sanskars without question, we honor their journey. Instead of resisting or rejecting them, we send them the energy of love and understanding.

Acceptance also opens the door to deeper **self-love** because when we accept others, we are also reminded that we, too, are worthy of acceptance. We're not perfect, and we don't need to be. We can be gentle with ourselves, knowing that we are constantly evolving, just like everyone else.

Creating Space for Serenity and Happiness:

In this space of acceptance, we find serenity, we heal, and ultimately, we allow happiness to flow freely within us. **When we accept what is, we make room for peace, growth, and love** to blossom—within ourselves, with others, and in every situation.

Comparison:

It's easy to forget that everyone is on their own unique journey, a journey that's not confined to just this lifetime but spans many births, countless experiences, and layers of sanskaras. We are all shaped by our past, the good, the painful, the lessons learned, and the unhealed wounds we carry with us. When we see someone else's path, it's tempting to compare it to our own, or to the path of someone else, as if there's a universal measure of success or happiness. But the truth is, each individual's journey is uniquely their own, and there is no standard blueprint that we all must follow.

The Danger of Comparison:

When we compare ourselves to others, or when we attempt to make someone else just like us, we **diminish their worth,** their uniqueness, and their personal struggles. We forget that they are

moving through their own experiences, shaped by the decisions they've made, the things they've lived through, and the karmic debts they're carrying. Every single one of us is walking with a **different set of beliefs, conditioning, and past experiences**, all of which are what makes us who we are.

No True Comparison Exists:

When we try to say that someone else is "better" than another, we inadvertently lower their **self-esteem**, because we create an illusion that they are somehow lacking. **But in reality, there is no comparison.** No one's path can be truly understood by anyone else. **We are all different,** and that difference is what makes the world so beautifully complex. Our job isn't to measure ourselves or others against a set of standards but to ask: **How can I be better today than I was yesterday?**

Each person does things in their own way. Some might have more experience, some may have more knowledge, and others may have had different opportunities. But **no one's journey is easier or harder than another's**, it is simply **their journey**. Every individual has their own input, their own time and energy invested, and their own karmic baggage that influences their decisions.

When we begin to recognize this, when we stop comparing and start **accepting each person's journey as valid**, we release the need for judgment. We stop trying to fit people into molds that aren't meant for them. Instead, we begin to see others with compassion, understanding that their choices are the result of their own personal history, and that **we each have our own timeline and path to follow.**

Honoring Individual Paths:

So let's stop measuring others by our standards and start focusing on how we can evolve, grow, and become the best version of ourselves. **Let us honor our differences and the unique paths that everyone is walking.** There's no race, no competition, just the simple and profound truth that we are all trying to find our way home in our own time, in our own way, and that's okay. And when we accept this truth, we free ourselves from the burden of comparison, and we create space for understanding, love, and mutual respect.

Powerful reflections on life and self-mastery:

"Anger is a punishment we give ourselves for someone else's mistakes."

When we hold onto anger, we are the ones who suffer. The person who caused the hurt may not even be aware, but we carry the burden of it. Letting go is not for them, it is for our own peace.

"Speak only when words are better than silence."

Silence has its own power. Not every thought needs to be spoken, not every reaction needs to be expressed. When we do speak, let it add value, bring clarity, or offer kindness. If not, silence is the wiser choice.

"Give what you want."

If we seek love, respect, or understanding, we must first give it. The energy we put out into the world is what comes back to us. What we withhold from others, we also deny ourselves.

"Sometimes in the middle of nowhere, you find yourself."

When we step away from the noise, the expectations, and the distractions, we discover who we truly are. In solitude, in unfamiliar places, in moments of stillness, we meet ourselves in ways we never could before.

"No one can hurt me. I use people's words to hurt myself."

Hurt is not in what others say but in how we receive it. When we stop internalizing negativity, we become untouchable.

"Life is a beautiful game that is very easy to play. It is we players who make it complicated."

Life itself is simple, it is our attachments, fears, and expectations that complicate it. When we let go, life flows effortlessly.

"One way to be light is to speak your mind. If something is not worth speaking, then it is not worth thinking."

Unspoken thoughts can weigh us down. Either express them or release them. Holding onto them only burdens the mind.

"When we have no expectations of others, we are programming ourselves to be in the present moment and we can respond proactively."

Expectations tie us to the past or future. Living without them frees us to respond with clarity and wisdom, instead of reacting with disappointment.

"My decisions in life are based on the values I have held. If my values are high, my decisions will always be right."

Decisions become clear when they align with our deepest values. Integrity in values leads to integrity in choices.

"If my priorities are set, it becomes easier to make decisions."

Clarity of purpose simplifies life. When we know what truly matters, decisions are no longer dilemmas. They are natural steps forward.

Happiness:

The Search for Happiness Within:

Your words touch a deep, universal truth about the pursuit of happiness. It's a truth we all carry within us but often forget in the chaos of life. We spend so much time looking for happiness, love, and peace in external things, chasing them as if they are somewhere outside of us, somewhere we can find and possess. But the reality is these qualities live inside us, waiting to be nurtured and cultivated.

When we react to the world with anger, blame, or hurt, we spill the very essence of what makes us whole, our inner peace, our joy, our contentment. We unknowingly give away what we need most. But it's a cycle, isn't it? We look for love, acceptance, and happiness in the world around us, forgetting that we have the power to create those feelings within.

Rediscovering Inner Power:

Just like the body needs balance among the five elements to thrive, our inner selves need balance among the seven qualities that define our true essence, qualities like love, compassion, peace, and joy. If even one of them is neglected, we begin to feel an emptiness, a longing that pushes us to seek it elsewhere. But the truth is that everything we long for, everything we search for, is already a part of us. It's not about finding it outside; it's about rediscovering it within, acknowledging that we have always held the key to our own happiness.

The real journey is not to search for happiness, but to create it, moment by moment, interaction by interaction. When we learn to embrace and nurture these qualities within ourselves, we become the source of the love and happiness we seek. The outer world doesn't need to be perfect; it's our inner world that needs to be in harmony.

It's never too late to begin creating this, to refill the glasses that have spilled. When we remember this truth, we reconnect with our own power, our own essence. That's when we can truly begin to feel the love, peace, and happiness that have always been within us.

The Trap of External Happiness:

We often find ourselves in the trap of believing that happiness is something we must acquire, something that only comes through external achievements, relationships, or validation. We think that once we achieve that goal, once we have that relationship, or once we acquire that success, we will finally be happy. But in this chase, we've overlooked the most important truth: happiness is not something we need to acquire; it is something we need to create within ourselves.

Neglecting Our Inner Self:

We've been so focused on filling the empty space with things outside of us, material possessions, titles, relationships, that we've neglected to nourish our inner selves, to create the happiness, peace, and love we seek in the only place that matters: within. By placing happiness as a distant destination, we've allowed ourselves to be consumed by jealousy, competition, anger, and hurt. These emotions don't bring us closer to happiness; they weigh us down, leaving us with strained relationships, anxiety, and a sense of emptiness.

It's like we've been sailing on the sea of life, believing that we need to keep acquiring more to reach a place of contentment. But what we don't realize is that, just like a ship, we can only carry so much. When we fill ourselves with negativity, resentment, and the constant need for more, we risk sinking, losing the very happiness, health, and peace we are seeking. We've been creating the very things that prevent us from feeling joy, and the cost of that journey has been so high.

What we create along the way, our thoughts, our actions, our emotions, becomes the final product of our lives. If we create negativity, competition, and harm, we will reap the consequences of those actions. But if we choose to create love, gratitude, and peace, then that's what we will experience. Happiness doesn't come from the destination; it comes from the journey. And if we live each moment with intention and compassion, we begin to realize that the happiness we were chasing was always here, waiting for us to embrace it.

What is important:

Your reflection strikes at the heart of what it means to truly live with intention and integrity. It's so easy to get swept up in the relentless pursuit of success, achievement, and external validation, but in doing so, we can lose sight of the most important things, the values that ground us, the inner peace that nourishes us, and the joy that comes from living authentically.

Centering on Core Values:

Reminding yourself to be happy first isn't selfish; it's an act of self-love and self-preservation. It's about choosing joy before the noise of the world pulls you in every direction. When you can center yourself on happiness, when you align with your core values, whether it's sincerity, honesty, respect, or love, you can navigate the world with clarity and confidence. The external world can be chaotic, filled with temptations and pressures to compromise. But when your internal compass is strong, decisions become easier, because you know that nothing is worth sacrificing your integrity or peace.

It's powerful to ask yourself: In the quest for achieving everything, am I losing something? This question is a reminder to pause, reflect, and ensure that your journey is in alignment with who you truly are. It's a call to make sure that in the pursuit of success, you don't lose the essence of yourself. If you lose your values, if you lose your self-respect, then what have you truly gained? Success without integrity is hollow; achievements without authenticity feel empty.

Clarity through Commitment:

When you know where your priorities lie, when you commit to living by your values no matter the circumstance, the path ahead becomes clearer. Decisions no longer feel like burdens but like affirmations of who you are. You don't need to compromise. If sincerity is your guiding star, then you can hold your ground, no matter what pressures or temptations come your way.

The True Measure of Success:

In the end, it's not the things we achieve or acquire that matter most, it's how we achieve them and the person we become in the process. By staying true to your values, you are not only creating success, but you are also creating a life filled with integrity, peace, and deep fulfillment.

It's true that happiness isn't something we can grasp from the outside, something we can acquire or hold onto. It is something we create from within, and it begins with our mindset, our feelings of contentment, and our ability to share and give without the fear of lacking.

Escaping the Trap of Scarcity:

If we constantly feel like we don't have enough, whether it's love, peace, joy, or resources, we become trapped in scarcity. We feel we have nothing to give because we are consumed by the belief that we are lacking. But the key is to shift that perspective. True happiness arises not from accumulating more, but from recognizing and appreciating what we already have. It's in the little moments, the simple things, the breath we take, the love we give, the peace we create within. When we are content with what we have right now, we free ourselves from the chains of constant seeking.

You're so right. If we depend on external things to make us happy, we're constantly at the mercy of variables that can change in an instant. But if we cultivate our happiness through good thoughts, through intention, through the choice to be content and kind, we tap into a power that is steady and unwavering. We can create joy even in the most difficult moments because we know it doesn't come from what's around us. It comes from within us.

Reclaiming Happiness: Creating Joy from Within:

The moment we realize that we are the creators of our happiness, we reclaim our power. Every thought we choose to nurture has the potential to bring us peace, love, and joy. We no longer have to wait for circumstances to change, for life to be "perfect" before we can be happy. Happiness is in our hands. It's in the way we choose to see the world, to embrace what we have, and to share it with others. When we choose to give from a place of abundance, from the contentment within, we not only enrich the lives of others but also deepen our own sense of fulfillment.

CHAPTER 11

IMPERFECT PEOPLE CREATE PERFECT RELATIONSHIPS

We live in times that seem full of chaos, unpredictability, and conflict, both in the world around us and within ourselves. The external world is fraught with natural calamities, social tensions, and turmoil, and the behaviors we encounter often reflect deep imperfections. It can feel overwhelming to witness so much pain, anger, and anxiety, and at times it seems as though we have lost touch with the peace and harmony that we so desperately need.

The Power of the Mind:

Yet, in the midst of this Kalyug, an era marked by conflict and confusion, there is a truth that remains unwavering: the state of our own minds is the one thing we can still control. Everything else seems to be in flux, but the power we have to choose our response, to create a space of peace and love within, is something that remains in our hands. It's not easy, though. So often, we are slaves to our own conditioning, our **sanskars,** our past habits and emotional patterns that drive us without us even realizing. These influences shape our thoughts, our reactions, and our perceptions of the world. But the beauty lies in recognizing this, in realizing that we don't have to be at the mercy of our past or our emotions. We can choose.

One of the greatest challenges we face is learning to accept people as they are, without judgment, without criticism. Our tendency to be critical, to find fault, to judge others, reflects a deeper inner struggle, a reflection of the unrest within our own minds. If we are constantly criticizing, we are not allowing ourselves to love. We cannot create one emotion while holding onto another. If we are living in a space of judgment and criticism, we are blocking the flow of love, peace, and compassion that is within us.

The Choice to Respond:

But in any given moment, we have the choice to change this. We can choose to create love, acceptance, and understanding. We can choose to see others with kindness, to offer them the space to be imperfect, as we are all imperfect in our own ways. When we stop focusing on what's wrong with the world, we create room for what is right within ourselves. Our ability to love, to forgive, and to heal.

Taking Back Control, One Thought at a Time:

In the face of so much uncertainty and pain, it is within our power to be the calm in the storm, the love in the midst of conflict. Our mind may seem like it's often out of control, but we can begin to take back that control, one thought, one choice at a time. By being mindful of our own thoughts and emotions, we can shift the energy we bring into the world and in doing so, help heal not just ourselves, but the world around us.

The Illusion of Changing Others:

When two people come together, their interactions are shaped by their sanskars, their past experiences and patterns. But instead of seeing each other's true essence, we see only what's been acquired, the layers of conditioning that often result in misunderstanding, resentment, or anger. It's so easy to fall into the trap of wanting the other person to change, to align with our expectations, but we forget one fundamental truth: both people want change, but no one is willing to give. In our desire to receive love, understanding, or peace, we end up withholding it, and this creates a vicious cycle.

The Cost of Projecting Negativity:

When we project anger, hatred, or criticism onto another, we leave ourselves feeling empty, depleted, and emotionally drained. Instead of offering the positive energy we so desperately need, we are consumed by negative emotions that only perpetuate the conflict. Both people feel as though they are waiting for the other to make the first move, but nothing changes because neither person is willing to be the source of healing. In the end, we wonder why things never improve, why the distance between us grows wider. The truth is that we were waiting for them to change, but we didn't realize that the change needed to come from within us.

The Cycle of Emotional Garbage:

Anger is like throwing garbage in a room. When we harbor negative emotions, we essentially fill our inner space with clutter and toxicity. And when we project that anger or criticism onto others, we not only damage our peace but also place the burden of that negativity on them. They, in turn, respond with their hurt, adding more garbage to their emotional room. And so, the cycle continues. One person's hurt feeds another's pain until we are all drowning in emotional garbage, never addressing the root of the issue.

Breaking the Cycle from Within:

The key to breaking this cycle is to become aware of our own emotional state and take responsibility for it. Instead of expecting the world and others to change, we must first look within. When we feel anger, instead of projecting it outward, we must pause and ask ourselves, "What is the source of this? What can I do to heal and let go?" The moment we stop blaming others for how we feel, we reclaim our power to create positive energy, to offer kindness, to nurture peace within ourselves and in our relationships.

Shifting Relationship Dynamics:

It is only by being the change we seek that we can begin to shift the dynamics around us. When we choose to offer love instead of judgment, understanding instead of criticism, we start to create a space of healing, not just for ourselves, but for the people we interact with. We stop waiting for the other person to change, and instead, we begin the process of healing within. Through this, we can slowly but surely dismantle the walls of hurt, criticism, and blame that we've built, and make room for connection, compassion, and growth.

Change starts with us. When we stop throwing garbage into the emotional room, we can begin to fill it with love, understanding, and positive energy. That is how we heal both ourselves and our relationships.

What is it that I could do to rectify this?

It's a painful but beautiful truth that when we question or judge another person's behavior, we are essentially rejecting them. We make them feel as though they don't belong, as though they are wrong for being who they are. But what if instead of judgment, we choose acceptance?

Acceptance as an Act of Love:

Acceptance is a powerful act of love. It is the ability to see another person's imperfections and still embrace them fully, understanding that everyone is operating out of their own sanskars, their unique conditioning, past experiences, and emotional makeup. When we come from a place of awareness, when we truly understand that each person's behavior is a reflection of their journey and struggles, we shift from rejection to acceptance. This doesn't mean we condone harmful actions, but rather that we approach them with understanding and acknowledging that, "Everyone is right in their own way." That doesn't mean we always agree with others, but it means we acknowledge their right to have their own perspective. The moment we radiate this energy of acceptance, it opens the door for connection. People become more willing to listen, to hear us, because they feel respected and understood. When we stop defending our own right to be "right" and instead listen with empathy, the entire dynamic changes. It becomes a space where both people can grow, learn, and move forward together.

Lowering the Racket:

In a tennis game, if both players are hitting the ball back and forth, the game continues. But the moment one person decides to stop, the game is over. In relationships, it's often one person's willingness to lower the racket, to stop defending their stance, that creates space for resolution. When we let go of our need to be right and allow the other person's viewpoint to be heard, the conflict can dissolve.

Discipline and Self-Transformation:

The more we practice acceptance, especially of other people's imperfections, the more we realize that, in doing so, we create the conditions for a perfect relationship. It's not about waiting for the other person to change; it's about changing our own approach. Just like in your analogy of cleaning the room, we cannot ask someone else to make changes if we haven't first looked at ourselves. To bring peace to our relationships, we must first find peace within ourselves.

Spirituality teaches us that transformation starts from within. When we apply the laws of love, compassion, and acceptance to ourselves first, only then can we extend them to others. We cannot discipline or change anyone without first disciplining and transforming ourselves. The practice of self-awareness and self-discipline allows us to show up in the world with love and understanding, ready to share that energy with those around us.

CHAPTER 12

THEORY OF KARMA

Every thought we have, every feeling we experience, and every action we take is the result of an ongoing process, a process that starts with the information we gather from the world around us. But what happens next is crucial: how we *feel* about that information, and how we *respond* to it. That response, especially when repeated, becomes our attitude. And as our attitudes solidify, they drive our actions, our **karma.**

External Karma: Actions as Expressions of Inner Patterns:

It's remarkable and, at times, unsettling to recognize how deeply our habitual thoughts and feelings can shape our personalities and behaviors. When we react repeatedly in the same way, those reactions become ingrained, and the external actions we take, like shouting or withdrawing, are simply the outward expressions of deeper internal patterns. This becomes our external karma—the actions we perform, which are visible to others.

The Cycle of Frustration:

Someone repeatedly making the same mistake and not listening to us is a powerful example. It's so easy to fall into the trap of frustration, to shout or act out, because we feel unheard, misunderstood, or even disrespected. And in that moment, shouting is our external karma. It's the action that comes from the feeling of being disrespected, and that action, when repeated, becomes a part of our personality, a habit, a reaction that defines who we are in that moment.

Breaking the Cycle:

But this process is not inevitable. We can stop and reflect. We have the power to shift the cycle. When we become aware of our thoughts, our feelings, and the resulting actions, we can start to consciously choose different responses. Instead of shouting, we can choose calmness. Instead of reacting with frustration, we can choose patience. Instead of criticism, we can choose understanding.

Transformation Begins Within:

It all begins with recognizing that our thoughts are not just passing whims, they are shaping our reality. Our feelings are not just fleeting emotions, they are the fuel for our actions. If we continuously react with anger, frustration, or fear, those reactions become a part of who we are. But if we choose peace, love, and understanding, then those will become the qualities that define us.

This is where true transformation happens, not in the external actions we take, but in the internal shift we create. When we change how we think and feel, we change how we act. And over time, we rewrite the story of who we are. We stop being slaves to automatic reactions and start becoming the conscious creators of our own karma.

In the end, it's not about blaming ourselves for the mistakes we've made, but about recognizing the patterns we've created and choosing to transform them. By changing our thoughts, our feelings, and our actions, we can create a new reality, one where love, peace, and understanding become our natural state, and where the karma we create is a reflection of our highest self.

The Mind as a Record Keeper:

It's truly astonishing how every moment, every action we take, every word we speak, and every thought we have is recorded, not just in the world around us, but within ourselves. Our minds, particularly the hippocampus, act as a vast storage bank, collecting and holding onto every experience, every emotion we've ever felt, and every instance of karma we've ever created. This means that the pain, joy, frustration, or love we felt in any given moment doesn't just disappear, it lingers, stored within us, ready to resurface whenever we are reminded of it.

Reliving the Past Through Emotional Memory:

We may think that karma is only what we do on the outside, but it starts much deeper when we revisit those memories, those "scenes," we don't just remember what happened; we relive the emotions we felt at the time. That is the essence of internal karma. It's not just about the physical actions we take; it's about the emotional residue we carry with us. Every time we think about a past event or interaction, we are re-creating the same emotions, replaying the same karma, and reinforcing the cycle of energy. This is what makes it so challenging to move on from past hurts or unresolved conflicts, it's not just the external action that we're stuck on; it's the internal emotional replay that keeps us trapped in a loop.

The Essence of Internal Karma:

But here's the powerful truth you've shared: karma isn't just about what we do. It's also about what we think. Our thoughts are energy. They shape our reality and, ultimately, our relationships. If we carry negative thoughts about others, even if we speak kind words or perform kind actions, the energy behind those words or actions will still carry a weight. The intention behind our karma, the true energy we bring to it, is what ultimately shapes the outcome. If our thoughts are not aligned with our actions, we create a disconnect.

This disconnect can cause inner conflict and strain the relationships we try so hard to maintain.

It's so easy to blame others for the way we feel or the circumstances we face. But the truth is, our reactions are always within our control. We may not be able to control what happens to us, but we can control how we respond. Every thought we create is a choice; every reaction is an energy we send out into the world. When we choose to reflect, to pause before reacting, we reclaim control over our karma.

The Uncontrollable Nature of External Karma:

The consequences of our actions, our external karma, are beyond our control. These are the energies from the outside world that come to us, and this is where destiny comes in. Destiny is not something that we can control; it is the result of the energies and actions of the world around us. But what we can control is how we respond to it, how we choose to think, and how we choose to act in the face of what life presents us.

In this way, we become the creators of our own reality. Not by controlling the world, but by mastering our own energy and reactions. And in doing so, we walk a path of conscious karma, of deliberate choice, where the energy we send out is one of love, compassion, and peace, shaping the world we live in.

Internal Karma / External Karma:

There is an intricate connection between our actions, the consequences they create, and the way we carry the emotional weight of those actions within us. The story about breaking a glass table and running away is a powerful example of how external karma, the physical act we take, creates a ripple effect that follows us far beyond the moment of action.

At that time, your action was quick, an instinctive response to avoid facing the consequences. But the emotional and mental consequences, the **internal karma**, that you created by choosing to escape the situation lingered. As you revisit the event in your mind, it's not just the broken glass that you see; it's the guilt, the regret, the grief for not taking responsibility. Every time you remember it, the same feelings arise, reinforcing the cycle of pain that follows us in life. That's the emotional burden we carry, the karma of unacknowledged actions.

When the Cause Is Forgotten but the Impact Remains:

But the powerful lesson here lies in the realization that karma isn't just about what happens immediately. It's about the consequences that unfold over time, sometimes even in ways we don't expect. Just like the broken glass that might lead to an injury later, our actions, even when seemingly small or insignificant at the time, can create lasting consequences in our lives. We may forget the cause, but the impact remains, and when those consequences come to us, whether it's an injury or any other form of hardship, we often find ourselves blaming others or life itself for the pain. We may scream in frustration, but in reality, we are carrying the weight of our own choices.

The Illusion of Blame:

We can continue to blame others for the pain we feel, or we can choose to take responsibility, to clear the broken glass. In your example, this is the moment of power, the moment when we have the opportunity to stop the cycle of blame and start taking control of our lives. By acknowledging our actions, by choosing to make amends, we reclaim our power. This act of responsibility is not just about fixing the external situation; it's about healing our internal world, too.

In every moment, we have a choice. We can continue to relive the regret and guilt of our past actions, or we can choose to take responsibility, to let go of blame, and to heal the emotional wounds that have followed us. The mind is indeed the only one that listens to us. When we choose to control our thoughts, to shift our perspective, we find the peace and power that were always within us.

Every Moment Shapes Our Destiny:

This is the essence of karma: the understanding that every thought, every action, every decision carries weight. The moment we take responsibility, we begin to clear away the broken glass, and in doing so, we create a space for healing and peace. Every action we take, every word we speak, every thought we create is not just a fleeting moment, it is a step in the journey of our lives, shaping our destiny in ways we may not always understand. In truth, the karma we create today has already set the course for the future, and in that sense, everything is **predestined.** But here's the beautiful and transformative realization: with every consequence we face, we have an opportunity to make a new choice, to write a new chapter in our lives.

The Sacred Opportunity of the Present Moment:

When we face the results of our past actions, we are not trapped by them. Instead, we are given a chance, a sacred chance, to act with full awareness and responsibility. We are not bound by the mistakes of yesterday, but empowered by the lessons they have taught us. **Now**, in this moment, we have the power to choose how we will respond. We have the power to write our destiny anew, to make decisions that align with our highest self, to take actions that reflect our true values.

The moment we act with awareness and responsibility, we are no longer passive victims of fate; we become active creators of our own future. This is where our true power lies, not in blaming the past or fearing the future, but in being fully present in the now, making conscious choices, and understanding that **each choice** we make is a brushstroke on the canvas of our life.

By choosing to take responsibility for our actions and their consequences, we are no longer just repeating patterns, we are transforming them. We are no longer repeating old karma, but creating new karma, filled with wisdom, love, and compassion. With this awareness, we start to shape a future that reflects the person we truly wish to become.

Destiny as a Living Creation:

So today, in every moment, we are writing our destiny with intention. With every conscious thought and action, we have the power to shift our path toward greater peace, joy, and growth. Our destiny is not something set in stone; it's something we have the privilege of creating with every choice we make, from a place of full awareness, love, and responsibility.

Let us embrace this power with all our hearts, knowing that in each decision, we are shaping not only our own lives but also the world around us.

The powerful metaphor of the boomerang perfectly captures the essence of karma: once it's set into motion, once the action is taken, we lose control over how it will return. The moment we make a choice, we are creating a ripple that will come back to us, and that ripple, those consequences, is the result of our own doing.

The Boomerang of Energy:

What makes this insight so profound is the understanding that whatever is happening to us, in this very moment, is not a random event or an unfair twist of fate. It's the result of the karma we have created, the boomerang we threw. And while we may not always understand the reasons behind what we face, we can know deep down that it is accurate. It is a consequence that has been set in motion by our own choices. This acceptance can be a source of deep peace. Instead of resisting life's challenges, we learn to see them as opportunities to reflect on the energy we have put into the world.

But there's more to this beautiful reflection: we always have a choice, even in the face of the consequences. The boomerang may return to us, but how we respond to it is entirely within our control. This is where our **internal karma** comes in. In any given moment, we have the power to choose how we will feel, how we will react, and how we will move forward. This is our internal karma, the thoughts, emotions, and choices we make in response to life's events.

Mastering the Inner Response:

Even when external circumstances are beyond our control, our internal responses remain ours to shape. Will we react with frustration, anger, or blame, or will we choose acceptance, understanding, and love? This is the key to transforming our lives. By consciously choosing our internal karma, we take ownership of our emotional landscape and begin to heal the emotional wounds that past actions might have created.

It's in our hands, always. The boomerang is always in motion, but how we respond to it is where we find our true strength.

The Power to Choose Anew:

What truly stands out in your reflection is the understanding that the past is not our prison. The past may present itself in our lives as pain or consequence, but it is only a stimulus, a prompt that is outside our control. What we do with it, how we respond, is the true power we hold in our hands. Every moment, every choice we make, is an opportunity to create new karma, to change the trajectory of our lives. That is the essence of our freedom: our ability to choose our present karma, regardless of the past.

If we don't change our karma today, if we don't choose to respond with love, compassion, understanding, or peace, then we will continue to relive the same pain, the same cycle. The past will bleed into our present, and the hurt we carry will only grow. It's as if we are trapped in a loop, where the past continuously defines our reality, and the present is no longer fresh or new but a repetition of what has already been.

The Power Lies in the Present:

This is where true transformation happens: when we realize that our focus should not be on changing the **destiny**, the body, the outer world, or the external circumstances, but on changing the **karma** we create today, in this moment. The stimulus, the consequences of the past may come, but how we respond is where our power lies. That is the only thing in our control.

This is the essence of personal growth: realizing that destiny, the outer world, and the consequences of past actions may shape our reality, but they do not define it. Our present karma, our actions, thoughts, and choices in this very moment is what shapes the future. It's in our hands to choose peace, to choose love, to choose healing. And as we do, the past starts to fade into the distance, and we create a future filled with the energy of our highest, truest selves.

I Radiate What I Create:

When you say that **karma changes, destiny changes,** it is a reminder that we have the power to transform our entire life by changing the way we think, feel, and act. What we create, we radiate and what we radiate, we attract.

Every thought we create is like a thread woven into the tapestry of our destiny. When you say, "I radiate what I create," it means that every thought, whether positive or negative, carries a frequency, an energy that we send out into the world. This energy, this vibration, then comes back to us, shaping the experiences we face. It's not just about what happens on the outside, but about how our inner world reflects and shapes our outer reality.

The emotional weight of this is heavy but necessary: if we do not recognize the power of our thoughts, they will continue to shape our actions and reactions. The more negative thoughts we harbor, the more negative energy we radiate, and the more we attract that negativity back into our lives. It's like an endless cycle, one that only deepens if we don't consciously break it. Thoughts are the seeds that create our karma, and if we continue to water the seeds of anger, resentment, fear, or doubt, those very seeds will grow into more negative consequences, perpetuating the cycle.

We Are the Architects of Our Destiny:

This is where true power lies: in our conscious awareness. Every thought we create is recorded not just in our minds but in our bodies. Our cells, every fiber of our being, are impacted by the energy we emit. That's why we must be so mindful of the thoughts we entertain, the information we consume, and the emotions we allow to take root. They shape us, not just mentally but physically, emotionally, and spiritually. When we allow ourselves to be bombarded by negativity, whether from external sources or our own minds, it wears us down, leaving us drained, exhausted, and disconnected from the peace we deserve.

We are the architects of our own destiny, and it all begins with the thoughts we choose to entertain. So let us be gentle with our minds, be discerning in the information we consume, and be vigilant in the thoughts we nurture. By doing so, we can create a flow of energy that lifts us, heals us, and transforms our world. The power to change our karma, to change our destiny, is in **our hands**. One thought at a time.

The Law of Return:

The metaphor of throwing a ball and knowing it will come back is such a powerful way to understand the essence of karma. The ball represents our actions, the energy we send out into the world, and just as we know that a thrown ball will return to us, every action we take will have a consequence. The key here is **awareness**. Being fully conscious of the fact that every choice we make is setting something into motion, and understanding that we cannot escape the return of that energy.

Once we throw the ball (take an action), we should not question or resist its return. Life's circumstances, the consequences of our actions, are simply reflections of the choices we made. When we question them, when we ask "Why is this happening to me?", we lose our focus and invite unnecessary pain. Instead of being in a space of acceptance and understanding, we become caught up in confusion and frustration. But when we approach life with awareness, knowing that our actions are leading to these consequences, we are prepared to receive them with calm and grace.

Choosing wisely, living with awareness of the impact our actions, words, and thoughts have, is the path to greater peace. And when we take responsibility, the soul recognizes its power. **The more we accept that we are choosing our reality**, the more we align with our highest self, and our soul becomes stronger, more resilient, and more in tune with the flow of life.

Visualization : Affects Brain and Body:

Harvard study on Visualization:

The idea that the brain cannot distinguish between actual experience and imagined experience is a powerful reminder of how much control we have over our minds and bodies, even when we are not physically engaged in an action. The fact that both groups, the one that physically played the piano and the one that only imagined doing so, showed the same changes in brain activityis a testament to the incredible influence that our thoughts and emotions have on our physical reality.

The example of Group A (external karma) and Group B (internal karma) is such a beautiful, emotional reflection on how our internal world shapes our experiences. Group A's experience was external. They physically engaged in playing the piano, creating action and karma in the world. But Group B's experience was internal. They imagined playing the piano with their fingers, and yet their brains and bodies reacted in the same way. This demonstrates just how powerful our thoughts are. Our minds don't just reflect the world around us, they create it. The internal karma, the thoughts and emotions we experience, has the same profound impact on our bodies and minds as external actions.

The Emotional Replay Loop:

This is where it becomes emotionally charged: when we relive an experience in our minds, especially one that was painful, we are essentially reliving the same emotions over and over again. Our brains don't differentiate between the past and the present, the real and the imagined. **Every time we revisit that pain, that hurt, or that anger, we are experiencing it anew**. This process **affects our bodies just as much as the original event**. It creates the same emotional and physical reactions, the same changes in the body, and can even lead to the creation of disease.

This internal dialogue, this constant replaying of negative thoughts, is so draining. We carry the weight of our past actions, our regrets, our anger, and our hurt, and these thoughts shape our present reality. When we do this repeatedly, our body starts to mirror the emotional stress, and the consequences are not just emotional, but physical.

Healing Begins in the Mind:

The truth here is powerful: we have the ability to shape our health, our happiness, and our well-being not just through external actions, but by **choosing** the thoughts we dwell on. We have the power to change our internal dialogue, to choose thoughts of peace, healing, and forgiveness, rather than rehashing old wounds. This is a deep call to awareness, to recognize that our minds are incredibly powerful creators, and every thought we hold shapes not only our reality but our health.

Healing, then, begins in the mind. By choosing to let go of the past, by choosing to forgive ourselves and others, we can free ourselves from the emotional cycles that keep us trapped in pain. The brain and body are deeply interconnected, and by shifting our internal karma, our thoughts and emotions, we can create a healthier, happier future. It's a reminder that we are not victims of our past or of our circumstances. We have the power to heal, to change, and to transform, through every thought we choose to think.

Beyond the Brain:

Our brains are not independent decision-makers; they are simply receptors, responding to the signals and instructions that come from a deeper source within us, the soul. The soul, the essence of who we truly are, is the one that sends forth the instructions, the energy, and the intention behind every thought, action, and emotion.

This truth touches on something profound about the nature of our existence: we are not just our bodies and brains. We are the soul, the eternal presence that directs and guides our experiences. The brain, then, is simply an instrument, a vessel through which the soul expresses itself. The signals it receives, whether they are thoughts of love or fear, joy or anger, are the messages sent by the soul. And these signals shape the very nature of our reality, impacting not just how we think and feel, but how we experience life itself.

This also means that the **power to choose** lies within us at a much deeper level. While the brain may not have the ability to choose, the soul is the true creator of our reality. It is the soul that holds the wisdom, the guidance, and the capacity to make choices that reflect our highest truth. When we align with the wisdom of our soul, we are in touch with the purest form of choice, one that transcends the limitations of the mind and body, and instead, is rooted in love, peace, and understanding.

What's so deeply emotional about this is the recognition that we are **not victims of our circumstances.** We are not mere passengers in our lives, subject to whatever comes our way. We have the **power to direct** our lives by tuning into the soul's guidance, by aligning with its highest vibrations, and by choosing thoughts, actions, and emotions that reflect our soul's true nature. The brain may be the instrument, but the soul is the conductor.

The more we connect with the soul's wisdom and embrace its guidance, the more we can take responsibility for the energy we put out into the world. This energy, emanating from the soul, is what shapes our experiences. Every choice we make, no matter how small, can be a reflection of our deepest self, the part of us that is eternal and unchangingand is connected to all that is.

Creator of our destiny:

In essence, we are always in control. Not by the brain, but by the **soul**. It is the soul that holds the key to transforming our reality, to healing our wounds, and to choosing love over fear, peace over chaos. This realization brings with it a deep sense of peace and responsibility: we are **the creators of our destiny.** We are not merely subject to what happens to us, we are actively co-creating our experiences with the energy we choose to radiate from within. And that energy, guided by the soul, has the power to heal, to uplift, and to transform not only our own lives but the world around us.

This understanding is deeply liberating, because it reminds us that no matter what the circumstances may be, we are always in touch with the **source of power within us.** The soul's wisdom is always available, always guiding us toward greater peace, love, and healing. All we have to do is listen.

CHAPTER 13

AWARENESS

What is it that a spiritual guru has achieved , the one thing for which we are all striving? Awareness is the light that guides us out of the shadows of unconsciousness. It's the key to peace, freedom, and personal transformation.

What's so emotional about this is the **empowerment** it brings. We are not at the mercy of our thoughts, our emotions, or our circumstances. **We are the creators** of our reality. When we are aware, we can ask ourselves those crucial questions:

- **What am I thinking?**
- **Is this thought serving me?**
- **Can I change it?**

And the most powerful realization of all: I am creating this. Every thought, every feeling, every reaction, it's all born from within us. The realization that we have 100% control over our thoughts is truly liberating. We no longer have to be victims of our emotions or mind patterns. Instead, we become conscious creators, able to choose the thoughts that align with peace, love, and wisdom.

Flowing with Life's Natural Rhythm:

This also brings us to such an important truth: Anything natural is peaceful. When we are in tune with our true self, when we are aligned with the flow of life, everything comes effortlessly, with ease and grace. But when we resist, when we try to force things, that is when the stress arises. Effort creates stress, but awareness creates peace. The more we tune into our thoughts, the more we recognize that they don't just come to us, they are born from our own minds. And that means we have the ability to shift them, to change them.

Awareness is the key to living a peaceful, empowered life. When we are fully present with our thoughts, when we take the time to reflect on them and ask ourselves, "Is this thought serving me?" we begin to unlock a deeper peace within us. We no longer need to chase happiness or solutions outside of ourselves. They are found in the stillness of awareness, in the quiet observation of our own minds.

This insight also reminds us that **we are not powerless**. We have the power to change our thoughts, and in doing so, we change our world.

This is an invitation to wake up, to become present, and to stop reacting unconsciously and start responding with awareness. Peace comes from within, and awareness is the path that leads us there. This message is a beautiful call to action, a reminder that we have everything we need to live a fulfilled, peaceful life right now, we just need to be aware.

Humility:

With a humble approach, we can guide others in a way that nurtures growth rather than resistance. True humility allows us to correct with kindness, making learning a shared journey rather than a confrontation. It's a beautiful thought, one that encourages us to lead with compassion and wisdom.

Surrendering the Ego:

When we demand change from others, we often do so from a place of ego. We raise our voices, assert control, criticize, believing that force will lead to transformation. But true change, the kind that touches hearts and lasts, does not arise from dominance. It flourishes in understanding.

Humility is the quiet strength that allows us to pause, to reflect on our own thoughts before we judge another's. It is the wisdom to recognize that our perception of "right" is shaped by our own experiences, and that others walk a path we may not fully understand. When we let go of our need to impose, to be "right," we create space for compassion.

Humility softens the barriers between us. It turns correction into guidance, disagreement into dialogue, and resistance into openness. When we surrender the ego, our words become gentle, our presence becomes healing, and our influence becomes effortless because it is no longer about control, but about love.

The Illusion of Identity:

It's the illusion we create around our identity, an illusion built on labels, roles, and societal constructs. We live our lives believing we are our name, our job, our nationality, our religion. But these are just external wrappings, layers we accumulate over time.

Who are we beyond these labels? If we strip away our titles, our professions, our affiliations, what remains? The truth is, our essence is something far deeper, something untouched by these temporary identities. Yet, we cling to them so tightly that any challenge to them feels like a personal attack. When someone speaks of our country, our faith, our status, we feel wounded because we have tied our sense of self to these labels.

But what if we could detach? What if we could see ourselves not as the wrapper, not as the jewelry box, but as the diamond within? The diamond does not change with time, roles, or circumstances. It simply shines, reflecting the light of truth, peace, and love.

Letting go of the ego is not losing ourselves. It is finally discovering who we truly are.

The Bindings of Ego:

Our ego binds us to fleeting emotions of superiority or inferiority, making us forget our true essence. When we identify with a role, a title, or a status, we become trapped in the illusion of self-importance or self-doubt. But beneath all of these external layers, we remain something much greater, a pure, conscious being.

True mastery is not about reacting to what others say or do, nor is it about attaching ourselves to transient identities. It is about recognizing that we are not just playing roles; we are beyond them. A true "Royal Being" is not someone with a title, but someone who governs their own mind with wisdom and stillness, unaffected by external praise or criticism.

The moment we react, we surrender our power. We become dependent on how the world sees us, rather than standing firm in the unshakable truth of who we are. But when we embrace our eternal self, free from ego's grip, we become untouchable. Radiating dignity, peace, and inner sovereignty.

The Vulnerability of Attachment:

Recognizing our sincerity is natural. It is a reflection of our true essence. But the moment we attach ourselves to this image, we become vulnerable to hurt. Suddenly, someone else's opinion has the power to shake us because it threatens the identity we have built around our sincerity.

True humility, however, frees us from this emotional turbulence. It allows us to understand that sincerity is not a fixed, universal measure. It is fluid, shaped by perspectives and capacities. What feels like dedication to me may not look the same to you, and that is okay. Humility is the wisdom to accept these differences without feeling diminished or defensive.

Letting Go of External Validation:

When we release the need for external validation, we no longer feel the need to prove ourselves. We simply are steady, secure, and at peace, knowing that our sincerity does not need to be measured against another's. It just exists, effortlessly, like the breath we take.

The essence of true humility is speaking not from ego or the need to control, but from a place of stability and care. When we correct or guide someone, it should not be to prove we are right or to make ourselves feel better, but purely for their benefit.

True humility means we do not impose expectations. We share wisdom, and then we let go. We do not wait anxiously for them to agree, change, or validate our words. Once spoken, it is complete, like a telegram, where every word is chosen carefully, concisely, and with purpose, because unnecessary words carry unnecessary weight.

When we communicate with humility, we do so with clarity, love, and detachment. We trust that if the other person is ready, the message will reach them. And if they are not, we remain at peace, knowing we have done our part.

CHAPTER 14

SLEEP

Sleep is more than just a break for our body, it's a **necessary process** for maintaining both our physical and mental well-being. The fact that sleep involves different stages, from light to deep, and even includes a period of vivid dreams during REM sleep, shows how our bodies and minds are constantly working, even when we are not consciously aware.

During sleep, we enter a state of unawareness. A time when our sensory activities are inhibited, and our motor reflexes subside. This is an emotional reminder of how we, as humans, have periods of **stillness** in our lives, where we can let go, relax, and trust that our bodies and minds are still doing the essential work they need to do—even when we are not actively engaged.

The sleep cycle is a beautiful representation of **balance. Non-REM sleep,** which is lighter and allows us to rest, and **REM sleep,** where dreams emerge and the mind processes emotions and experiences, remind us that both rest and introspection are necessary parts of our emotional and mental healing. In life, too, we experience cycles of rest and reflection, where we might feel more at ease and relaxed during some phases, and more deeply introspective during others. Both stages are essential.

And in the end, just as our body goes through cycles of sleep, NON-REM and REM, the emotional and mental cycles in our lives are necessary too. Each stage serves a purpose, just as each sleep cycle helps us recharge and recover. In those quiet, restful moments, our brain is engaged in deeply meaningful work, and this is a reminder that even when we feel like we are "doing nothing," we are in fact processing, healing, and growing.

This teaches us to honor the importance of sleep, but also to **honor the cycles in our lives.** Just as we need deep rest for physical and mental restoration, we also need emotional and mental rest for true healing. We sometimes forget that our minds, like our bodies, need time to heal and recharge. This reminder to **trust the process** and honor these cycles is deeply comforting and empowering.

Why do people sleep?

The question of why we sleep holds such a deep and emotional truth at its core. Sleep is not just a physical necessity; it is a sacred time of restoration for our bodies, minds, and spirits. When we sleep, we are not only resting but also actively renewing ourselves, much like how nature recharges the earth after a storm.

Energy conservation and storage happen while we sleep. We are constantly giving our energy to the world around us, whether it's through work, relationships, or simply navigating the challenges of life. But sleep teaches us that it's okay to slow down, to recharge, to pause, and to fill ourselves up again. There is wisdom in rest, a reminder that we are not meant to be in constant motion, that sometimes, the best thing we can do for ourselves is to simply be still and let our energy be replenished.

Self-repair and recovery that occur during sleep speak to our inherent capacity to heal, physically, mentally, and emotionally. How beautiful it is to know that while we sleep, our body is working tirelessly to **mend** itself, to heal the wounds, the fatigue, the stress we experience throughout our days. Just as a flower closes its petals at night and reopens in the morning, our body and soul undergo a silent **recovery,** finding balance and peace within.

The Healing Power of Sleep:

But perhaps most touching of all is the idea that brain development and maintenance occur during sleep. Our minds are constantly at work, storing memories, processing emotions, and making sense of the world. Sleep provides a space for healing our minds, for sorting through the chaos of the day and finding clarity. In this peaceful state, our brains can develop and grow, just as we do emotionally and spiritually. Sleep is a time when we are allowed to be vulnerable, to let go of the burdens of the day, and to trust that our minds will work through everything we've encountered, even when we aren't consciously aware of it.

Sleep teaches us to be kind to ourselves, to know that true strength comes not only from doing, but from resting, restoring, and trusting in the wisdom of our own bodies. It's in those moments of stillness that we truly grow.

What happens during NREM?

Stage 1 of sleep is such a beautiful, tender moment in the journey of rest. It's the phase where we gently let go of the world around us, a quiet invitation for our bodies and minds to surrender to peace. As our heartbeat slows, our breathing softens, and even the tiniest movements in our eyes settle, we are gently cradled into the quiet of sleep.

It's a moment of **grace**, the brief time when we transition from the chaos of the waking world to the sanctuary of rest. Just 10-15 minutes, but in those precious moments, there's a deep sense of **letting go,** of releasing the weight of the day, allowing ourselves to be **fully present** in the now, without needing to do anything.

Stage 2 of sleep is where we truly begin to sink into deep peace, where the world outside starts to feel more distant, and we are enveloped in the quiet embrace of rest. As our heartbeat, breathing, and muscle activity slow even further, it's as if our body is whispering to us: "You are safe. You are at ease. You can completely relax now."

In these moments, as our body temperature drops and our brain waves settle, it's a gentle reminder of the **power of stillness**, that in the slowing down, we find true healing. This is the stage where we allow ourselves to **unwind** completely, to let go of the stress, the tension, and the worries that we carry through our waking hours. It's a time to release the weight of the day and to allow our bodies to recover and replenish in a way that words cannot describe.

The fact that we spend about half our sleep in this stage speaks volumes about the **balance and restoration** happening within us. Stage 2 is like a **quiet, protective cocoon,** wrapping us in comfort and peace, ensuring we have the space to rebuild and renew.

In this stage, the body knows what it needs. It doesn't need to do anything, it just needs to **be**. And in that "being," there's so much power and healing. It's as though in this moment, we are **perfectly aligned with the rhythm of life,** where everything slows down and harmonizes, bringing us back to ourselves.

Stage 2 sleep isn't just about physical rest. It's about returning to a state of inner peace, where we can heal and rebuild, one breath, one beat of the heart at a time.

Stage 3 of sleep is where the magic of true healing and regeneration takes place. It's a profoundly emotional moment when our bodies and minds are given the deepest kind of restoration. As our heartbeat, breathing, and muscle activity reach their lowest, and our brain waves slow even further into the deep, powerful rhythm of delta waves, we enter a space where regeneration isn't just a process. It's a sacred act of self-care.

In this stage, the body is working tirelessly behind the scenes, releasing **growth hormones** that help repair tissues, muscles, and bones. Every cell in our body is receiving the nourishment it needs, and the **immune system** strengthens, like a quiet guardian protecting us from within. Even our **memory** is being nurtured, the moments of our lives, our learnings, and experiences quietly settling into the safe corners of our mind, ready to be accessed when we need them.

Deep sleep, Stage 3, is also when the body **regulates** so many vital functions, like glucose metabolism and hormone release, reminding us of how **interconnected** everything truly is. This sleep is a time of profound **balance,** where the body and brain are brought back to equilibrium, and even the slow oscillations of our brain waves work to synchronize and create harmony in every part of us. It's a beautiful dance of healing, one that is gentle yet incredibly powerful.

The fact that we are less receptive to outside stimuli during this stage is a testament to the incredible protection our bodies have in place for these critical moments of regeneration. It's as though, in this deep, sacred sleep, we are given the space to heal without any distractions or interruptions. And though we may experience a grogginess if we're awakened during this time, it's simply because our bodies are still processing and absorbing the profound healing that has taken place.

Stage 3 sleep is a quiet reminder of our body's incredible **capacity to heal,** to regenerate, and to restore itself when given the time and space to do so. It's as though every part of us is being renewed in this stage—physically, emotionally, and mentally. This is the deep sleep that reminds us of the **power of rest**, and how it's not just sleep, but a **gift** of regeneration and healing. In this time of **slow wave sleep,** we find ourselves not only rejuvenated but also reconnected to the very essence of **life**. The quiet rhythm of restoration that we so deeply need.

REM sleep is a truly fascinating and emotional stage of rest—a time when we truly connect with our inner worlds in the most vivid and powerful way. It's the stage where dreams come alive, where our minds are free to explore, create, and process the emotions and experiences we've had while awake. During this time, our eyes move rapidly behind our eyelids, a visual reflection of the intensity and activity of the dreams we are experiencing.

What's so profound about REM sleep is that even though we are at rest, our **brain activity mirrors that of being awake.** It's as if our minds are actively working, untangling the emotions, thoughts, and experiences we've encountered during our waking hours. This stage of sleep allows us to process, **reflect,** and **heal** in ways we might not fully understand. It's a time for **emotional resolution**, where our dreams help us make sense of things, relieve emotional burdens, and perhaps even guide us toward a deeper understanding of ourselves.

REM sleep accounts for about **25%** of our total sleep time, and during this period, our minds are working overtime, creating stories, making connections, and sometimes even offering us answers or insights through the dream world. The fact that the first REM cycle is shorter, but each one that follows lengthens, is a reminder that the deeper we go into sleep, the more our **minds** and **souls** need to process and integrate.

In these moments, the boundaries between waking and dreaming blur, and we enter a sacred space of **transformation**. A time when we are given the opportunity to heal, release, and grow. Dreams that occur during REM sleep are not just random images, but often deeply connected to our **emotions,** our **fears,** and our **hopes**. They are like emotional **whispers** from the subconscious, guiding us toward a better understanding of our inner selves.

This stage is so powerful because it serves as a reminder that even in our rest, we are always **working** on ourselves, processing, healing, and reconnecting with the deepest parts of who we are. And even though we might not always remember our dreams, the experience of **REM sleep** is an intimate, emotional journey that allows us to release, restore, and move forward with greater clarity and emotional peace.

NREM sleep, particularly the deep stages that occur at the beginning of the night, is absolutely essential for our physical and emotional well-being. It's in this phase that our bodies and minds undergo the crucial recovery and restoration we need to thrive. The way our brain uses less energy during NREM sleep, while also strengthening and organizing memories and new skills, is like a quiet, gentle rebuilding process. It's as though our mind is preparing us, tidying up the pathways so we're ready to face the world again when we wake up.

This deep sleep is the moment when our physical recovery truly happens. It's in these precious minutes that our blood pressure drops, our body rests, and the immune system gets the support it needs to heal and recharge. These moments of stillness allow our body and mind to heal from the physical and emotional strains of the day. The parasympathetic nervous system, which represents our body's natural state of calm and relaxation, is activated, guiding us into a deep state of peace and renewal.

When we wake up refreshed after a full night of NREM sleep, we are not just physically rested, but emotionally and mentally restored. The consolidation of memories, the strengthening of neural pathways, and the tidying up of our thoughts allow us to begin each new day with a sense of clarity and readiness as if our mind is perfectly attuned to the present moment.

There is something deeply emotional and nurturing about this process. It's like the universe has designed a system within us that allows us to reset, renew, and heal every single night. NREM sleep isn't just about the absence of consciousness. It's about deep rejuvenation. It's the foundation upon which our memories are built, our bodies are healed, and our minds find peace. In the quiet of NREM, we are given the opportunity to recover, reflect, and emerge stronger, more prepared for the challenges of the next day.

So, next time we find ourselves drifting off to sleep, we can rest assured that we are embarking on a deeply healing journey, one where the body and mind are gently recharged and realigned, ready to step back into the world with a renewed sense of **strength and peace.**

REM sleep is deeply transformative, both for our body and mind. During this stage, our muscles experience complete atonia, a form of paralysis that allows our mind to roam freely without the interference of physical movement. This is not a time of stillness or passivity, but one of intense cerebral activity. While our voluntary muscles are immobilized, allowing our body to rest, our emotional brain center comes alive. It's here, in this delicate balance of stillness and activity, that dreams emerge, beautiful, mysterious, and sometimes even healing.

What makes REM sleep so extraordinary is the way it **supports our emotional well-being**. As the brain processes the emotions we've experienced during the day, it creates a space for **healing.** Whether we are consciously aware of it or not, this stage of sleep helps us **integrate** and **process emotional experiences,** especially the difficult or traumatic ones. This is why **dreams** often serve as a way to make sense of what we're feeling, offering insights into our subconscious mind. It is as if the mind is giving us a chance to work through our emotions, so we wake up lighter, more at peace.

REM sleep also plays an essential role in learning. During this phase, our brain is not just passively resting. It's actively organizing and absorbing. This stage allows our memory centers to soak up information, to consolidate those new inputs in our long-term memory, and to analyze and evaluate them, leading to greater wisdom. This is where knowledge evolves into understanding.

Through REM sleep, our brain isn't just storing facts, but it's building wisdom, the kind of deep, intuitive knowing that comes from synthesizing information and experiences. We don't just learn things in a linear way, but we integrate them into our broader understanding of life, and this can lead to solution-focused thinking and clarity in times of challenge.

But perhaps one of the most emotional aspects of REM sleep is the way it supports **emotional healing.** When we sleep, especially during REM, we are given the opportunity to **reset** and **reboot** our emotional state. After a day filled with highs and lows, our mind and body find balance, helping us move past emotional trauma. It's like a gentle process of **emotional cleansing,** allowing us to let go of negativity, heal past wounds, and wake up feeling renewed and ready to face the day with fresh perspective and energy.

The importance of REM sleep cannot be overstated. It is not just the stage where we dream. It is the stage where we **heal, grow,** and **learn.** It's the time when our emotional and cognitive systems work together to process, integrate, and help us move forward with a clearer, stronger, and more peaceful mind. In this quiet, active space, we find the ability to heal from trauma, learn from our experiences, and emerge each morning with the strength to face whatever comes next. This is the true power of REM sleep. Nurturing the mind, body, and soul in a way that no other stage can.

Sleep and Mental Health:

The amygdala, as the emotional center of the brain, is responsible for processing our emotions, especially fear and anxiety. When we don't get enough sleep, the amygdala becomes overactive, leading to heightened emotional responses that are difficult to control. It's like our emotional center gets supercharged, and our reactions become quicker and more intense. Without enough rest, the prefrontal cortex, the part of our brain that brings logic, reason, and calmness, loses its ability to regulate these heightened emotions.

The example of the gun pointed at you is so vivid. It shows how the amygdala and the prefrontal cortex work together to assess a situation, with the amygdala triggering an immediate emotional response, and the prefrontal cortex deciding how to act on that. When we're well-rested, this system works in harmony. We can stay calm, make rational decisions, and manage our emotional responses.

But when we're sleep-deprived, this balance is disrupted. The amygdala becomes hyperactive, while the prefrontal cortex struggles to maintain its logical control. Small irritations, like someone speaking loudly on the phone, can turn into triggers for frustration or anger. We may find ourselves reacting in ways that don't truly reflect the situation, simply because our brain hasn't had the time to recharge and reset.

It's such an emotional reminder of the importance of sleep, not just as a physical necessity, but as the foundation for emotional balance. Our minds need rest, just as much as our bodies do, to maintain peace, clarity, and calmness. When we prioritize sleep, we allow our emotional reactions to stay in check, enabling us to approach life's challenges with more patience and understanding. It's a powerful call to action for all of us to take care of our sleep, for it is through this rest that we find the strength to navigate our emotions and the resilience to stay centered in the face of life's stresses.

Emotional Memory:

Our childhood memories, both the joyful and the painful, are stored in a part of our brain that carries the rawness of emotions. Over time, as we recall these memories, we notice that the intensity of the emotions they once held is often softened, like a faded photograph. This is where sleep, especially REM sleep, steps in and does its delicate work of emotional healing.

When we dream during REM sleep, our brain engages in a powerful detoxification process, separating the emotions from the memory itself. It's as though the brain knows that we cannot move forward carrying the weight of unresolved emotional baggage. By disconnecting the intense emotions from these memories, we are able to experience them more objectively, without being overwhelmed by them. In a way, it's a beautiful form of emotional therapy that happens every night while we sleep.

The process is truly awe-inspiring. During REM sleep, our brain releases neurotransmitters like acetylcholine, which help to solidify the memories we've made while awake, and this is when both the hippocampus (our memory center) and the amygdala (our emotional center) are actively engaged. This creates a perfect environment for emotional healing. The intensity of our emotional memories is tempered, and over time, they lose some of their power to hurt us.

But what happens when we don't get enough REM sleep?

It's heartbreaking to realize that sleep deprivation leads to emotional upheaval, and the consequences are more severe than we may think. By day 5, the absence of REM sleep can lead to signs of psychosis, an intense breakdown of emotional stability. This highlights just how essential sleep is in maintaining our emotional equilibrium.

It's incredibly moving to think about how our brain, through the wisdom of sleep, works to heal our emotions and help us process the weight of life's experiences. The idea that every night, our brain is actively taking care of us, detoxifying emotional memories, and giving us the peace we need to face each new day, is a profound reminder of how interconnected our mind, body, and spirit truly are. Sleep is not just a time for rest. It's a time for healing, for recovery, and for emotional renewal.

REM sleep is the perfect condition for overnight emotional therapy.

REM sleep deprivation causes increased emotional upheaval and by day 5, they show signs of psychosis.

Dreams

Dream is a replay of your past memory and the time frame is long. Dream is any report of mental activity on awakening. Dream happens during REM sleep when we have bizarre hallucinations, vivid narratives, emotionally filled story experiences.

In dreams, we become psychotic.

1. We are hallucinating: when we dream we see things that are not there
2. We are delusional: we believe things that could possibly be untrue.
3. We are disoriented: We get confused about time, space, place, person
4. We are emotional: We are fluctuating vividly through our feelings, which are labile.
5. We have amnesia: when you wake up, you forget your dream.

If, while awake, we had experienced any of the above five, we would have been seeking psychiatric treatment. And despite that, what we are experiencing is a normal biological, psychological, absolutely necessary life-support set experience to go through.

In REM sleep, the areas that are active are:

Hippocampus – Memory-related area

Amygdala and ACC – Emotion-related area

Occipital lobe – Visual projections.

Prefrontal Cortex – (logic brain) shows depressed activity during sleep.

That's why dreams have visual experiences filled with eye movements, memories, and emotions, and are bizarre and irrational. The dream is a thing that your brain is telling you, this is essential stuff that you need to work through.

When we silence our conscious mind, subconscious memories of the past can emerge in our dreams. If we pay attention, we can resolve many unresolved issues. Most of our unresolved emotional hurts and injuries will keep coming up in our dreams, giving us an indication that the issue needs to be dealt with.

The initial part of our sleep is NREM, and the latter part is REM sleep.

REM sleep is important for emotional strengthening. If we have been working on our inner engineering, we will be able to reduce the need for REM sleep and manage to have fewer hours of sleep as we have been taking care of our emotional strength.

CHAPTER 15

REALITY: THE ULTIMATE TRUTH

Knowledge, as we know, is powerful, but it's not enough just to receive it or memorize it. It must be lived, practiced, and integrated into the very fabric of our daily existence. Until we apply that knowledge, until we take it beyond intellectual understanding, it remains just an idea, a concept.

The metaphor of churning milk to receive butter is so profound. Knowledge is like that milk, full of potential but needing to be processed through contemplation, reflection, and practice to truly become something nourishing, something that can sustain us. Until we churn it, until we test it and challenge it, it doesn't become our own. Only through consistent effort, through the act of incorporating that wisdom into our actions, do we experience its true power and its transformative potential.

What moves me about this is the realization that the wisdom we seek is already within our reach. It's not a distant goal or something we have to search for outside ourselves. It's about turning inward, questioning what we know, and testing it against the reality of our lives. When we do this, when we finally integrate that knowledge into our actions, we begin to see the true results of our learning. This is when knowledge turns into wisdom, and wisdom, in turn, shapes our lives in ways that are meaningful, purposeful, and deeply fulfilling.

We've all experienced this truth at some point in our lives. We may have learned something intellectually, but it was only when we put that learning into practice that we saw the true impact. The truth is not just what we know, but what we live. And when we live our truth, when we embody the knowledge we have gained, we witness the deep and lasting transformation that follows.

It reminds us that we are not just recipients of information; we are active participants in the process of our own growth. We must take that knowledge and turn it into something real, something that feeds our soul, nurtures our spirit, and shapes our destiny. That's when it becomes our property, when it becomes a part of us, and when it finally begins to change our world.

It's so easy to judge a situation or a person based on outward appearances, the richness, the success, the material achievements. We see someone with money or status and we think, "Wow, how lucky they are!" But as you so wisely point out, we are only seeing a fraction of the reality. Behind every external success is a deeper story, one that often involves stress, sacrifice, and untold struggles.

In a world that often feels focused on acquiring, on hoarding, on gaining more, the true richness of life is in what we give away. Whether it's love, kindness, time, or resources, giving to others is not just an act of generosity; it's a profound way to align with the universe. When we choose to uplift others, to help, to serve, we are rewarded not just with material blessings, but with a sense of peace, fulfillment, and grace that no amount of wealth can bring. The universe responds to the energy we put out. It mirrors back to us the vibrations we emit. If we choose to send love, positivity, and goodwill, that is exactly what we receive in return.

And here's the most powerful realization: Our eyes only show us part of the story. The truth is far more intricate, far more beautiful than what we can see with our physical eyes. When we look beyond the surface, when we learn to see with our "third eye", with spiritual awareness and deeper understanding, we realize that everything in life is interconnected. We begin to see the invisible threads of karma, the unseen forces that shape our experiences, and the limitless potential of our choices.

We are not our bodies, not the identities we carry, but the pure essence that resides within. It speaks to the core truth that when we realize the nature of our soul, we are liberated from all fear, attachment, and insecurity. We live in a world that constantly pushes us to accumulate, to possess, to hold on tightly to what we have. But what if we could truly understand, as this wisdom reminds us, that we came into this world with nothing and will leave with nothing? And yet, in the process, we have everything we need within us.

Desire brings a sense of loss, and true joy comes from simply allowing things to unfold for the first time. When we let go of expectations and desires, we step into the beauty of the present moment, where everything is new, fresh, and full of possibility. We no longer live in the constant ache of wanting or regretting. We are simply here, now, fully alive. In this state of non-attachment, we are truly free.

And then, there is the wisdom of silence, the power of stillness. It's in this silence that we can hear the truth of who we are. It's in this stillness that we reconnect with the divine energy that flows within us. The world around us is often noisy, chaotic, and filled with distractions, but when we quiet our minds, when we let go of the endless search for answers, we come home to ourselves. In that silence, we discover that we are not separate from the divine; we are the divine. We are consciousness and bliss in its purest form.

Everything is energy. The energy we create and direct within ourselves shapes our reality. And when we align with the flow of this inner energy, when we allow ourselves to be in harmony with the stillness and peace within, we step into the power of creation. We are the power generators, and the direction of this energy is ours to choose.

When we fully understand this, we stop searching for fulfillment outside of ourselves. We stop fighting, fearing, crying, and feeling insecure. We understand that we are already complete, already whole. This is the ultimate truth. When I embrace this truth, I am at peace with myself and the world. I no longer feel the need to grasp, to chase, to hold on. I can simply be. And in this being, I find everything I have ever sought. This is the power of silence. The power of stillness. The power of simply being. In this, we discover the present moment's bliss, the soul's peace, and the truth of who we are. We are Shiva. We are eternal. And in that knowing, we are free.